ALLEN TATE

THE HOVERING FLY AND OTHER ESSAYS

Essay Index Reprint Series

 BOOKS FOR LIBRARIES PRESS

FREEPORT, NEW YORK

809
T21h

ACKNOWLEDGMENTS are due the publishers of
the following, in which these essays severally have appeared:
The Sewanee Review, *The Virginia Quarterly Review*, *The American Scholar*, *The New English Review*, *On the Limits of Poetry* (The Swallow Press & William Morrow & Company), *New Verse*, *This Quarter*, *The Hudson Review*, *The Johns Hopkins Symposium on Criticism* (Bollingen Series, Pantheon Books), and *Inventario*.

INTERNATIONAL STANDARD BOOK NUMBER:
0-8369-0923-2

LIBRARY OF CONGRESS CATALOG CARD NUMBER:
68-22948

74-1281

PRINTED IN THE UNITED STATES OF AMERICA
BY
NEW WORLD BOOK MANUFACTURING CO., INC.
HALLANDALE, FLORIDA 33009

TO MAX WOLF

TABLE OF CONTENTS

A

THE HOVERING FLY
A Causerie on the Imagination and the Actual World

OF THE three great novels of Dostoevsky *The Idiot* has perhaps the simplest structure. In the centre of the action there are only three characters. The development of the plot is almost exclusively "scenic" or dramatic; that is to say, a succession of scenes with episodic climaxes leads, with more than Dostoevsky's usual certainty of control, to the catastrophe at the end. There is very little summary or commentary by the author; here and there a brief lapse of time is explained, or there is a "constatation," a pause in the action in which the author assumes the omniscient view and reminds us of the position and plight of the other characters, who are complicating the problem of the hero. I emphasize here the prevailing scenic method because at the catastrophe the resolution of the dramatic forces is not a statement about life, or even about the life that we have seen in this novel: the resolution is managed by means of that most difficult of all feats, a narrow scene brought close up, in which the "meaning" of the action is conveyed in a dramatic visualization so immediate and intense that it creates its own symbolism. And it is the particular symbolism of the fly in the final scene of *The Idiot* which has provided the spring-board, or let us say the catapult, that will send us off into the unknown regions of "actuality," into which we have received orders to advance.

What is *The Idiot* about? In what I have said so far I have purposely evaded any description of the novel; I have not tried to distinguish the experience which it offers, a kind of experience that might start a wholly different train of speculation upon actuality from that which will be our special concern in these notes. But now, before we get into the last scene, where the three main characters find themselves in a dark room, alone for the first time, we must drop them, and go a long way round and perhaps lose our way on a road that has no signs at the forks to tell us which turn to take.

II.   When we say poetry *and* something else—poetry and science, poetry and morality, or even poetry and mathematics—it makes little difference in dialectical difficulty what the coördinate field may be: all problems are equally hard and in the end they are much the same. The problem that I shall skirt around in these notes is a very old one, going back to the first records of critical self-consciousness. Aristotle was aware of it when he said that poetry is more philosophical than history. Although the same quagmire awaits us from whatever direction we come upon it, the direction itself and the way we tumble into the mud remain very important. Perhaps the crucial value of the critical activity —given the value of the directing mind, a factor that "systematic" criticism cannot find—will be set up or cast down by the kind of tact that we can muster for the "approach," a word that holds out to us a clue.

Armies used to besiege towns by "regular approaches"; or they took them by direct assualt; or they manœuvred the enemy out of position, perhaps into ambuscade. These strategies are used today, for in war as in criticism the new is usually merely a new name for something very old. When Cæsar laid waste the country he was using a grand tactics that we have recently given a new name: infiltration, or the tactics of getting effectively into the enemy's rear. When you have total war must you also have total criticism? In our time critics are supposed to know everything, and we get criticism on all fronts. Does this not outmode the direct assault? When there are so many "problems" (a term equally critical and military) you have got to do a little here and a little there, and you may not be of the command that enters the suburbs of Berlin.

At any rate the world outside poetry, which continues to disregard the extent that it is also *in* poetry, resists and eludes our best understanding. When and why did it begin to behave in this way? When we had the Truce of God for three days a week, we attacked, with a great deal of military rhetoric and pageantry, the enemy, on the fourth day, and the attack was a frontal assault; both sides knew the rules. But we do not know them. And in the critical manual of war there has been nothing comparable to the rules since Arnold's doctrine of the "criticism of life" could still engage the non- or anti-poetic forces of the world head on.

But suppose there isn't an enemy? Suppose the war figure is misleading? Henry James (one of the great critics) wrote to Stevenson in 1891 that "No theory is kind to us that cheats us of seeing." What did he mean? In this instance he meant Stevenson's refusal to visualize his scene. "It struck me," says James, "that you either didn't feel—through some accident—your responsibility on this article quite enough; or, on some theory of your own, had declined it." We know that Stevenson did have a theory that made him generalize his scenes.

It is not necessary to find out here what Stevenson missed, or what, missing that, he did actually succeed in seeing. Every imaginative writer has a theory, whether he recognize it or not; it may operate for him at some dynamic level where it can liberate all that writer's power; but in so far as it participates in the exclusive nature of theory, it must entail upon some phase of his work very great risks, even perils. "Thus Hardy," says William Empson, "is fond of showing us an unusually stupid person subjected to very unusually bad luck, and then a moral is drawn, not merely by inference but by solemn assertion, that we are all in the same boat as this person whose story is striking precisely because it is unusual." The "solemn assertion" in Hardy and in many other writers, critics no less than novelists and poets, must always either limit or somehow illegitimately extend what the writer has actually seen.

What I want to end these beginning remarks with is an observation that has been too little acknowledged. The art of criticism must inevitably partake of the arts on which it lives, and in a very special and niggling way. I refer to the "approach," the direction of attack, the strategy; and in terms of the strategy of this occasion, I mean the "point of view," as Percy Lubbock understands that phrase when he tells us that very nearly the whole art of fiction is in it. From what position shall the critic, who is convinced that the total view is no view at all, the critic not being God, and convinced too that even if (which is impossible) he see everything, he has got to see it from somewhere, like the painter Philippoteaux who placed himself under a tree in his picture of the Battle of Gettysburg to warn you that what you see is only what he sees, under that tree: under what tree, then, or from what hill, or under what log or leaf, shall the critic take his stand, which may be less than an heroic stand, to report what he sees, infers, or merely guesses? Merely to ask this question is enough to indicate something of the post which I am trying to find and hold. You may locate it far to the sinister side of the line which divides the arts and the sciences. Even if this spectator succeeds in holding his ground, you may be sure that he will not be able to give you a scientific report.

III. Suppose we take two terms and relate them. The two terms for this occasion are, first, Poetry, and, second, the Actual World. Do we mean then by the actual world a world distinguished from one which is less actual or not actual at all? I suppose we mean both things; else we should say: Poetry and the World. We might again alter the phrase and get: Poetry and Actuality, which by omitting the world would give us a clue to its bearing in the preceding phrase; that is, world might then mean region, realm, field of observation or experience. So I take it that the bearing of the phrase "actual world" is towards something outside us, something objective, whose actuality is somehow an empirical one which tends to look after its own affairs without consulting us, and even at times resisting whatever it is in us which we

like to call by names like subjective, private, human as opposed
to non-human, although even the human and the subjective lie
ready for objective scrutiny if we change our vantage-point and
let them stand opposite us rather than let them oppose a third
thing, a world, beyond them. It is, in fact, no mere quibble of
idealism if we decide to call this subjective field not only the
world but the actual world, taking our stand on the assumption
that it sufficiently reflects or gathers in or contains all that we
can ever know of any other world or worlds that appear to lie
beyond it.

Are we prepared to take this stand? Perhaps we are if we are
philosophers of a certain logical stubbornness; but as poets our
zeal for subjectivism might seem to be good only at times, at
certain places and moments. And are we, here in this kind of
enquiry, either philosophers or poets? To ask that question is to
diminish or perhaps to reduce to zero any degree of confidence
that we may have enjoyed in trying to sort out, however provisionally, some of the bearings of our phrase "actual world."
When we are sorting them out are we outside them, or inside,
or partly inside and partly outside?

If we go back for another glimpse of a suggestion that I merely
threw down at the outset of this discussion,
we shall drop to a degree somewhere below
zero in our confidence of certainty in this enquiry. From what position is the critic looking at the object of his enquiry? That was our
suggestion, but we have now identified the
critic's object as the actual world, whatever
that is, as that world is related to poetry, whatever that is.

If I seem to be making this matter obscure,
let me plead my ignorance, and if you will,
add your own ignorance to my plea; or if you like it better, add
your scepticism to mine; and we shall examine together our
riddle, so far as we can, as if nobody had seen it before: which,

I take it, is the *action* of scepticism as distinguished from the mere feeling of the sceptic.

I suppose the easiest and, for all I know, the best way to estab-lish our post of observation to look at the actual world, under our given condition, is to look at it through poetry. But here a-gain we encounter difficulties as harassing as those we almost had to give up when we plumped ourselves down into the actual world. Even if we knew what poetry is, we should have to find it in particular poetic works: you see in that abstract phrase—particular poetic works—how difficult it is to face the paralyz-ing simplicity of our problem at this stage. We should have to find poetry in poems. Does not that make it look easier? It does, until we remember that even the man who may have read five thousand poems, an anthologist, for example, could lay claim to real mastery of not more than a few hundred.

What, then, is poetry? The innocence of the question ought to excuse it. Were we German idealists of the past century, or their disciples of today, we might easily begin poetry with a cap-ital P, and putting initial capitals before actual and world, start Poetry and the Actual World off on their historic merry-go-round; or perhaps Poetry could pursue the Actual World as the Lord, in the Gullah sermon, chased Adam and Eve "round and round dat Gyarden, round and round"; or again there are the stock clowns in the bestiary of the animated cartoon that chase each other's tail until at last all that is left on the screen is a whirling vortex. Any of these similes will do that testifies to our helplessness before the fenced-in apriorism of the merely philo-sophical approach: its conclusions are impressive and are u-sually stated at length, but I have never seen one of them that increased my understanding of the twenty-eighth Canto of the *Paradiso*, or even of *Locksley Hall*.

But if we cannot say philosophically what poetry is, or even how it functions, how shall we know from any point of view what post of observation we are taking when we decide to look at the actual world through poetry? From now on this is what

I shall be trying to get at. We shall certainly not be looking on
as a spectator who has no stake in the scene; and yet to say that as
a man who has written verse I have a special tact which will lead
me to the right hill and turn my eyes in the right direction smacks
a little of our national reliance upon expert testimony. For even
if a poet, some other poet, seems in his verse to have given us
flashes of what we may provisionally call actuality, he is not, as
he talks about poetry, inside his verse, but outside it; and his
report is as much under the obligation to make good as yours.

IV.   I am sorry to introduce another complication before we go
further. I must introduce a broader term, and the broader term
usually lifts the spirits for a brief span, until somebody reminds
us that it may be an evasion of the harder distinctions enjoined
by the narrower term. The broader term is Imagination. If we
say that we are trying to discover the relation between the Imagination and the Actual World, we find ready to run to our aid
a host of comforting saws that could easily turn this vacillating
discourse into an oration—and may actually do so before we are
done. The Imagination is superior to Reality. Imagination is
the rudder, Fancy the sails. Imagination is the esemplastic power. There are others as good, perhaps even better; and I do not
deny the probability that before I am through I shall have spok-
en in substance one of these doctrines.
    Yet I have brought in the Imagination for a more empirical
reason. The great prose dramatists and novelists are makers and
thus poets, and they give us something that is coherent and moving about human life which partakes of actuality but which is
not actuality as it is reported to me by my senses as I look about
me at a given moment. How does their report differ from mine?
How does it differ from the report of the poet who writes, either
lyrically or dramatically, in verse? Perhaps we had better take
the risk and decide that the two reports seem to differ, verse being the occasion of the difference but not its explanation; and yet
bearing in mind a few of the examples and comparisons which

I shall produce or refer to in a few minutes, I make a large reservation about a categorical difference between the imagination in prose and the imagination in verse: Whether verse be expressive or formal in its function, it nevertheless becomes a sort of medium through which the poet may convey a deeper and wider heterogeneity of material than the prose vehicle will ordinarily carry. My reservation about this difference simply acknowledges the probability that it may be only a difference of degree, of intensity, of scope, with respect to the material; or if it is a real distinction, it cannot be said to hold all the time, but only as a rule. I admire, for example, the late Robert Bridges' poetry, but I see in it a failure or, if you will, a refusal to go all the way for as much of the richness of image as his magnificent control of verse-technique would have justified. On the other hand, if you will recall the cutting up of the whale in *Moby Dick* you will see at once the long reach of a prose style that is probably richer and more fluent than any verse style of its century, and far more dynamic than the style of *Dawn in Britain*, which perhaps alone in nineteenth-century poetry equals *Moby Dick* in rhetorical ambition. Bridges and Melville, then, might be seen as the exceptions in their respective mediums; and yet, in order to see them that way, we should have to establish a middle point at which the prose imagination and the verse imagination pass each other on the way to their proper extremes; and no such point exists except in books on the differential calculus.

But if we look at this matter empirically, not claiming too much for any differences or for our more confident distinctions, we may succeed in taking up an attitude towards a very real problem; for I take it that nobody denies the value of what seems to go on in sound works of the imagination. In what respects does this value belong to an actual world? In that spirit, we may phrase the question more narrowly, even finically, and ask it in terms of motion or process, or as Mr. Kenneth Burke would have it, of drama. In what ways, then, does an actual world *get into* the imagination?

Thus I turn to another line of speculation, with an observation that ought to arrest some of the vacillation of my opening trial
flights, and at the same time fix our point of view. If we think
of the actual world as either a dead lump or a whirling wind
somewhere outside us, against which we bump our heads or
which whirls us around, we shall never be able to discover it: we
have got to try to find it in terms of one of our chief interests. Let
us call that interest the imagination.

V.   There is now raging in one of our best journals a controversy
about a human crisis which the editors of that journal call "The
Failure of Nerve."* The full implications of the controversy   * *Part*
are irrelevant to the end of my discussion; yet there is one issue,   *vol. x,*
perhaps the central issue, of that controversy which may instruct
us, or at any rate prepare us for what follows. Professors Dewey,
Hook, and Nagel are anxious and at moments even a little angry
about the disorderly rebirth of certain beliefs about man that
tend to reject scientific positivism and the reliance upon what
they, in their tradition of thought, are pleased to call reason. The
answers to these challenging blasts are scarcely developed; the
editors of *Partisan Review* have so far relegated them to their cor-
respondence columns; and I do not know whether or not there
will be more considered replies. As an old anti-positivist I cannot do less than to point out a standard objection to the positivist
program, reminding its adherents that our supposed "failure
of nerve" might actually turn out to be the positivists' failure to
allow for all that our nerve-ends are capable of taking in.
    The positivist program for the complete government of man
may perhaps be a form of what Scott Buchanan has called
"occultation," a term that I should apply to positivism somewhat as follows: Positivism offers us a single field of discourse
which may be briefly labelled as physicalism; and it pretends
that this is the sole field of discourse, all the others being illusion,
priestcraft, superstition, or even Nazism. Now as this single
field of discourse is directed towards works of the imagination

it carries with it a certain test of validity, which is usually the semantical test; and I hold that when this test becomes the prag‑matic test and usurps the business of other tests, from other fields of discourse, pretending to be the sole test, it is performing an act of occultation upon these tests—a hiding away, an ascription of dark motives, even an imputation of black art.

Is there failure of nerve in a recognition of the failure of posi‑tivism even at its subtlest level to deliver all the goods? Are men the victims of a failure of nerve if, standing on a precipice from which there is no retreat, they prepare to make the best jump possible, and refuse to mumble to themselves that their fall will only exemplify the laws of gravity? There is no doubt that the fall will offer this confirmation of positivism; for positivism is a highly efficient technique of our physical necessities; it is the creation of the practical reason which organizes our physical economy, without which we cannot live. But under the rule of a positivism which has become a group of self‑sufficient sciences, the organization has grown exclusive. What is it that is exclud‑ed? What is *occulted*?

There are two answers to this question which are two ways of giving the same answer. But before I try to give this single‑double answer I ought to say that my purpose here is not to be‑rate the sciences but only the positivist religion of scientists. I am even more concerned with what it leaves out, or at least to "point" towards that omitted thing, as one nods in the direction of a good landscape which one might have missed, driving by it at seventy miles an hour.

What is excluded, what is occulted? First, the actual world; second, Dostoevsky's hovering fly; I shall be saying presently that in terms of the dramatic imagination the world and the fly are the same thing. Our scepticism—and as I say it I have my own doubt—our doubt of this identification proceeds from what we ordinarily call our common sense, a good thing to have, but not good enough if it is all we have. Let me put the matter some‑what differently. We may *look* at the hovering fly; we can to a degree *know* the actual world. But we shall not know the actual world by looking at it; we know it by looking at the hovering fly.

I am sorry that this sounds a little gnomic; and it is time to remember James' remark again: No theory is kind to us that cheats us of seeing. But it is also time to amend James: No theory is kind to us that cheats us of seeing what path we ought to be on. What is our path? When we do not know, we may get a vision, and then hope that all visions appear on the road to Damascus. Before we may build our hope so high we had better confront Pascal: "We run carelessly to the precipice, after we have put something before us to prevent us seeing it."

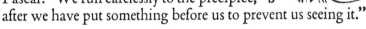

VI.   The fly appears out of nowhere in the last scene in *The Idiot*: out of nowhere, but only if we limit our apperception of place to the scale of the human will. There are, as I have said, three persons in the scene, but one of them is dead, and her place is taken by the hovering fly. Nastasya Filippovna has appeared less directly in the action than other women characters of the story; but she is the heroine; for it is she who creates for the hero his insoluble problem. She is a beautiful and gifted orphan of good family who has been seduced by her guardian, a libertine of high social and political connections at the court. There is Rogozhin, who, as the story opens, has just inherited a fortune; he is in love with Nastasya and he offers her the worldly solution of money and marriage, a solution that she will not accept; and it is he, of course, who murders her at the end, since in no other way may he possess her. From the beginning Prince Myshkin, our hero, has been in his special way in love with Nastasya. He is the "idiot," the man whom epilepsy has removed from the world of action. I am not prepared to add to our critical knowledge of Myshkin. He has a marvellous detachment and receptivity, and a profundity of insight into human motives which I believe

C

nobody but Dostoevsky has ever succeeded so perfectly in rendering dramatically. (It is always easy for the novelist to *say* that a character is profound; it is quite another matter to dramatize the profundity, to make it *act*.) Nastasya's agony of guilt, the conviction of sin, mirrors an almost Christ-like perception of the same potentialities on the part of Myshkin; and it is Nastasya who creates Myshkin's problem. Nastasya is tortured by those oscillating extremes, personal degradation and nobility of motive; and Myshkin alone in his world knows that she is not a "bad woman." But she will not marry Myshkin either. Marriage to Myshkin would be the symbolic signal that the pressure of her conflict had abated, and that Myshkin's problem had found solution in Nastasya's solution of her own. She cannot marry Rogozhin because she is too noble; she cannot marry Myshkin because she is too degraded. Thus we get in Rogozhin's murder of Nastasya the deeply immoral implications of Rogozhin's character, and the dramatically just irony of the good in her being destroyed by the lover who was indifferent to it. When the murder is done, Myshkin feels no resentment: he can accept that too. The lovers stand over the dead body of the murdered girl:

[*Myshkin's*] *eyes were by now accustomed to the darkness, so that he could make out the whole bed. Some one lay asleep on it, in a perfectly*

motionless sleep; not the faintest stir, not the faintest breath could be heard. The sleeper was covered from head to foot with a white sheet and the limbs were vaguely defined; all that could be seen was that a human figure lay there, stretched at full length. All around in disorder at the foot of the bed, on chairs beside it, and even on the floor, clothes had been flung; a rich white silk dress, flowers, and ribbons. On a little table at the head of the bed there was the glitter of diamonds that had been taken off and thrown down. At the end of the bed there was a crumpled heap of lace and on the white lace the toes of a bare foot peeped out from under the sheet; it seemed as

*though it had been carved out of marble and it was horridly still. Myshkin
looked and felt that as he looked, the room became more and more still and
death-like. Suddenly there was the buzz of a fly which flew over the bed
and settled on the pillow.*

   I assume that the minimum of exposition
is necessary; it is one of the great and famous scenes of modern
literature; and I hope that seeing it again you recalled the immense drama preceding it and informing it and stretching the
tensions which are here let down, eased, and resolved for us. I
am not sure that the power of the scene would be diminished by
the absence of the fly; but at any rate it is there; and its buzz rises
like a hurricane in that silent room, until, for me, the room is
filled with audible silence. The fly comes to stand in its sinister
and abundant life for the privation of life, the body of the young
woman on the bed. Here we have one of those conversions of
image of which only great literary talent is capable: life stands
for death, but it is a wholly different order of life, and one that
impinges upon the human order only in its capacity of scaven-
ger, a necessity of its biological situation which in itself must be
seen as neutral or even innocent. Any sinister significance that
the fly may create in us is entirely due to its crossing our own
path: by means of the fly the human order is compromised. But
it is also extended, until through a series of similar conversions
and correspondences of image the buzz of the fly distends, both
visually and metaphorically, the body of the girl into the world.
Her degradation and nobility are in that image. Shall we call it
the actual world?

  Or is there another adjective that we could apply to this world?
There doubtless is; but I cannot, for my purpose, find it short
of an adjectival essay, which this essay largely is, of another sort.
With some propriety we might call it *an* actual world, which
resembles other worlds equally actual, like Dante's or some of
Shakespeare's, in its own final completeness, its coherence, depth,
perspective. Yet I suspect that this side of the very great men we
seldom get magnitude with actuality. We get magnitude in

Thackeray and actuality in James; but not both in either. We get both in Tolstoy; but I take it that we accept his magnitude because it is actual, not because it is large. Thackeray's hurly-burly over the Battle of Waterloo is pleasant, empty, and immemorable; Prince André lying wounded under the infinite sky is all the world so lying; and we suspect that Tolstoy's magnitude is only a vast accumulation of little actualities—young Rostov on his horse at the bridgehead, the "little uncle" serving tea to the young people, Natasha weeping over Anatol in her room.

Whither do these casual allusions take us? They might take us far, on some other occasion, at a time when we had the heart for the consideration of actual worlds. But now we are in an occult world, from which actualities, which in their nature are quiet and permanent, are hard to find. As we face the morning's world we see nothing, unless we have the peculiar though intermittent talent for it, so actual as Dostoevsky's fly or Prince André's empty heavens. For if the drift of this essay have anything of truth in it, then our daily suffering, our best will towards the world in which we with difficulty breathe today, and our secret anxieties, however painful these experiences may be, must have something of the occult, something of the private, even something of the wilful and obtuse, unless by a miracle of gift or character, or perhaps of history also, we command the imaginative power of the relation of things.

VII.   It is a gift that comes and goes; its story is so long that neither time nor understanding has permitted me to tell it here. Yet I think that the risk, the extreme risk that I have so far faced, of some general commitments concerning the function of the imagination as a black art will be worth taking, if only to challenge a fierce denial. It ought to be plain to us, who share a common experience of two conflicts in a single war and who continue to wonder at the ingenious failure of our time, that although human powers are by no means depleted, something has gone wrong with their direction. No man but acknowledges this commonplace; yet how shall we imbed it, ground it, in some conceivable knowledge of the actuality of a world?

It must be plain also that the very instruments of our daily economy have more and more dictated our ends, or at best have suggested to an obscure power within us how we shall conduct our lives. The possibilities latent in our situation must make us falter. The obscure power within us we have made into an occult power; we are no longer conscious of its limits, its function, its purposes. Is that not the meaning of an occult power? One that we sway under but cannot know?

Here again I come up against formidable hazards, and I feel as if I had gone round the flank only to lose direction and to be cut off; but these perils will be plain enough although I shall not describe them. This occult power that seems to overwhelm us must, in times past, have enjoyed the fulness of light; but even underground it will not be gainsaid. If it does not have the privilege of its rational place in the order of human experience, it will take irrational toll of that order. Human violence is an historical constant; yet how shall we come to terms with a violence that is rationally implemented, an efficient, a total violence? It seems to me that the answer of our time to this problem is at present the historical answer of the dead-end, of the stalemate, of the facile optimism of decay. In a time like ours you may be sure of this: that men will be easy and hopeful, and will try a little of the medicine of the bridge-expert along with the elixirs of the innumerable Gerald Heards. Why? Because, although historically man may be a social being before he is a religious being, he is, after he achieves society, primarily religious, and remains incurably so. If he is told that mere "operational techniques" will see him through, whether these are put to work in society, or in the laboratory, or in industry, or in the arts, he may believe it for a while, and try to realize it; but like a child after the game is over and the fingers are uncrossed, he will return to the real world, unprepared and soon to be overwhelmed by it, because he has been told that the real world does not exist.

Or perhaps you would prefer to call it merely another world, after the analogy of *an* actual world; not *the* other world and *the* actual world. For there must be a great many of these worlds, all actual, all to be participated in, all participating in us; yet I prefer the frank Platonism of *the* actual world, as Socrates him-self preferred it when he told Ion that "poetry is one." And the impulse to reality which drives us through the engrossing im-age to the rational knowledge of our experience which, with-out that image, is mere process, must also be one. Once more the professed sceptic of thirty minutes ago reaches an immoder-ate deduction beyond any preparation that he has been able to ground it in.

For I should be chagrined could I feel that I have carried you, as well as myself, beyond known depths: are we not committed to the affirmation that actuality and poetry are respectively and even reciprocally one? If we are so committed, we must not affirm otherwise of humanity, which has been one from the be-ginning. And we cannot allow any novelty to our attempted insights.

Are we not saying something very old when we assert that we may know an actual world in the act of seeing the hovering fly? We are saying that our minds move through three necessities which, when in proper harmony and relation, achieve a dy-namic and precarious unity of experience. Now that our oration is over I may say quite plainly that the three necessities—neces-sities at any rate for Western man—are the three liberal arts. And any one of them practiced to the exclusion of the others retires a portion of our experience into the shadows of the occult, the contingent, the uncontrolled. The grammarians of the modern world have allowed their specialization, the operational tech-nique, to drive the two other arts to cover, whence they break forth in their own furies, the one the fury of irresponsible abstrac-tion, the other the fury of irresponsible rhetoric. The philosopher serves the operational technique, whether in the laboratory or on the battlefield. The poet—and the poet is the rhetorician, the specialist in symbol—serves the operational technique because, being the simplest mind of his trinity, his instinct is to follow and to be near his fellow men.

In a last glance at the last scene of *The Idiot* let us imagine that Myshkin and Rogozhin do not appear. The body of Nastasya Filippovna lies indefinitely upon the narrow bed, the white toe exposed, the fly intermittently rising and falling over the corpse. The dead woman and the fly are a *locus* of the process of decomposition. But, of course, we cannot imagine it, unless like a modern positivist we can imagine ourselves out of our humanity; for to imagine the scene is to be there, and to be there, before the sheeted bed, is to have our own interests powerfully affected. The fiction that we are neither here nor there, but are only spectators who, by becoming, ourselves, objects of grammatical analysis, can arrive at some other actuality than that of process, is the great modern heresy: we can never be mere spectators, or if we can for a little time we shall probably, a few of us only, remain, until there is one man left, like a solitary carp in a pond, who has devoured all the others.

—1943

THE NEW PROVINCIALISM
with an Epilogue on the Southern Novel

A NOTE written around a subject needs a formidable title to remind the writer where he is going and to make the elusive subject a little clearer to the reader. I confess to feelings of peculiar inadequacy on this occasion; it reminds me of a similar occasion ten years ago, when I was writing an essay for the tenth anniversary number of *The Virginia Quarterly Review*. That essay (as I recall it: I have not been able to bring myself to reread it as I begin to write)—that essay was possibly a little stuffy and more certain of itself than these notes can be. It was written at the height of the Southern literary renascence. That renascence is over; or at any rate that period is over; and I write, we all write, in the time of the greatest war. Will the new literature of the South, or of the United States as a whole, be different from anything that we knew before the war? Will American literature be more alike all over the country? And more like the literature of the world?

An affirmative answer to the last question would make our literary nationalists—Mr. Van Wyck Brooks, Mr. Kazin, and Mr. De Voto—look a little oldfashioned, very much as they have actually been all along as the intellectual contemporaries of Buckle and Taine. Their influence is no longer very much felt by anybody who seriously writes; and it is sufficient here merely to state the paradox that not even literary nationalism could abort a genuine national literature when it is ready to appear; when in fact we become a nation. But it is more likely that we may become an internation first. These reflections are set down to prepare for something that I have long wanted the occasion to say: that mere regionalism, as we have heard it talked about in recent years, is not enough. For this picturesque regionalism of local color is a byproduct of nationalism. And it is not informed enough to support a mature literature. But neither is nationalism.

Yet no literature can be mature without the regional consciousness; it can only be senile, with the renewed immaturity

of senility. For without regionalism, without locality in the sense
of local continuity in tradition and belief, we shall get a whole
literature which Mr. John Dos Passos might have written: perhaps a whole literature which, in spite of my admiration for Mr.
Dos Passos' novels, I shall not even be able to read. This new
literature will probably be personal, sentimentally objective,
tough, and "unsocial," and will doubtless achieve its best effects
in a new version of the old travel story (like most of Mr. Dos
Passos' books, which are travel stories) both abroad and at home:
the account of voyages to the South and West, and to the ends
of the world. New Crusoes, new Captain Singletons, new
Gullivers will appear, but Gullivers who see *with*, not *through*
the eye. It will not be a "national" literature, or even an "international"; it may be a provincial literature with world horizons,
the horizons of the geographical world, which need not be spiritually larger than Bourbon County, Kentucky: provincialism
without regionalism.

II.   If regionalism is not enough, is a world provincialism enough?
It has been generally supposed in our time that the limitations of
the mere regional interest, which are serious, could be corrected
by giving them up for a "universal" point of view, a political
or social doctrine which would "relate" or "integrate" the local
community with the world in the advance of a higher culture.
What this higher culture is or might be nobody was ever quite
clear about. It looked political, or at any rate "social," and it
ranged in imaginative emphasis all the way from the Stalinist
party line, upon whose front, in this country, was written the
slogan, Defense of Culture *(whose culture?)*, to Mr. Wallace's
Common Man, whom Mr. Wallace seemed willing to let remain common.

What it never occurred to anybody to ask was this simple
question: What happens if you make the entire world into one
vast region? This, it seems to me, is the trouble with our world
schemes today: they contemplate a large extension of the political

and philosophical limitations of the regional principle. "Let's get closer to the Chinese." "Know your fellow men, and you will like them better, and cease to fight them." Are these propositions true? I doubt it. Europeans are fighting one another today not because they didn't "know" one another. It does not, of course, follow that they are fighting because they did know one another; but that proposition makes as good sense as its contrary. For the real end is not physical communication, or parochial neighborliness on a world scale. The real end, as I see it, is *what* you are communicating after you get the physical means of communication. It is possible for men to face one another and not have anything to say. In that case it may occur to them, since they cannot establish a common understanding, to try to take something away from one another; and they may temporarily establish, as they did a generation ago, certain rules of mutual plunder that look for a time like "international coöperation."

All this has a bearing on literature today, the literature of the United States, and of the South, in the recent past and in the near future. For the logical opposite, or the historic complement, of the isolated community or region is not the world community or world region. In our time we have been the victims of a geographical metaphor, or a figure of space: we have tried to compensate for the limitations of the little community by envisaging the big community, which is not necessarily bigger spiritually or culturally than the little community. The complement of the regional principle, the only force which in the past has kept the region (of whatever size) from being provincial, from being committed to the immediate interest, is a non-political or supra-political culture such as held Europe together for six hundred years and kept war to the "limited objective." That is to say, there was sufficient unity, somewhere at the top, to check the drive of mere interest, and to limit war to a few massacres prompted by religious zeal or by the desire of rulers to keep their neighbors from getting out of hand. The small professional army at the top never tried to use and thus to menace the vast, stable energy of the masses, until the age of Louis XIV; and it was not until Napoleon that it was thought possible to make a whole nation fight.

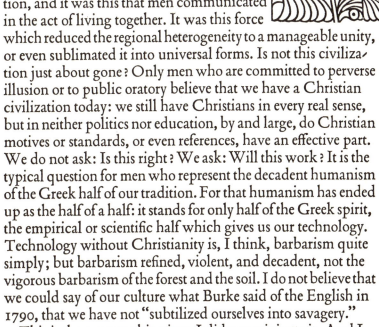

The kind of unity prevailing in the West until the nineteenth century has been well de-scribed by Christopher Dawson as a peculiar balance of Greek culture and Christian oth-erworldliness, both imposed by Rome upon the northern barbarians. It was this special combination that made European civiliza-tion, and it was this that men communicated in the act of living together. It was this force which reduced the regional heterogeneity to a manageable unity, or even sublimated it into universal forms. Is not this civiliza-tion just about gone? Only men who are committed to perverse illusion or to public oratory believe that we have a Christian civilization today: we still have Christians in every real sense, but in neither politics nor education, by and large, do Christian motives or standards, or even references, have an effective part. We do not ask: Is this right? We ask: Will this work? It is the typical question for men who represent the decadent humanism of the Greek half of our tradition. For that humanism has ended up as the half of a half: it stands for only half of the Greek spirit, the empirical or scientific half which gives us our technology. Technology without Christianity is, I think, barbarism quite simply; but barbarism refined, violent, and decadent, not the vigorous barbarism of the forest and the soil. I do not believe that we could say of our culture what Burke said of the English in 1790, that we have not "subtilized ourselves into savagery."

This is the catastrophic view. I did not originate it. And I suppose it cannot be wholly true. A few men will still somehow evade total efficiency, and live much as they did in the past; many will be bored by machines or, like the retired banker in my community, refuse to use their products by making by hand the articles of daily utility. The individual human being will probably have in the future as in the past a natural economy to which he can occasionally return, if he is not meddled with too much by power at a distance.

This natural economy cannot be an effective check upon the standardizing forces of the outside world without the protection of the regional consciousness. For regionalism is that consciousness or that habit of men in a given locality which influences them to certain patterns of thought and conduct handed to them by their ancestors. Regionalism is thus limited in space but not in time.

The provincial attitude is limited in time but not in space. When the regional man, in his ignorance, often an intensive and creative ignorance, of the world, extends his own immediate necessities into the world, and assumes that the present moment is unique, he becomes the provincial man. He cuts himself off from the past, and without benefit of the fund of traditional wisdom approaches the simplest problems of life as if nobody had ever heard of them before. A society without arts, said Plato, lives by chance. The provincial man, locked in the present, lives by chance.

III. It must be plain from this train of ideas whither I am leading this discussion. For the world today is perhaps more provincial in outlook than it has been at any time since the ninth century, and even that era had, in its primitive agrarian economy, a strong regional basis for individual independence. Industrial capitalism has given us provincialism without regionalism: we are committed to chance solutions of "problems" that seem unique because we have forgotten the nature of man. And having destroyed our regional societies in the West, we are fanatically trying to draw other peoples into our provincial orbit, for the purpose of "saving" them.

Our Utopian politics is provincial. It is all very well to meet at Dumbarton Oaks or on the Black Sea to arrange the world, but unless the protagonists of these dramas of journalism have secret powers the presence of which we have hitherto had no reason to suspect, the results for the world must almost necessarily be power politics, or mere *rules of plunder which look like coöperation.* The desired coöperation is for the physical welfare of man. But it is a curious fact (I have not been able to find any history which denies the fact) that the physical welfare of man, pursued as an end in itself, has seldom prospered. The nineteenth century dream of a secular Utopia produced Marxian socialism, National Socialism, and the two greatest wars of history; and it is perhaps only another sign of our provincialism that we ignore the causation between the dream and the wars, and urge more of the same dream to prevent other wars which the dream will doubtless have its part in causing. Nobody wants to see the Oriental peoples dominated by the Japanese and going hungry and ill-clad; yet so far in the history of civilization it has been virtually impossible to feed and clothe people with food and clothing. It is my own impression that they get fed and clothed incidentally to some other impulse, a creative power which we sometimes identify with religion and the arts.

It is small game; yet are not the Four Freedoms a typical expression of our world provincialism? Here is a radio fantasy on the secular dream of the nineteenth century. We guarantee to the world freedom of thought—to think about what? (I had supposed we were opposed to freedom of thought for the Germans and the Japanese.) Is it freedom to think *our* thoughts? We guarantee to the world freedom of worship—to worship what? Unless you cut the worship off from everything else that the Javanese, the Hottentots, the Russians, and the Americans may be doing (in our own case we have almost succeeded in this), what is to keep the Javanese, the Hottentots, the Russians, and ourselves from worshipping a war-god and putting this religion to the test of action? We guarantee to the world freedom from want. We had better—or somebody had better guarantee it, even if the guarantee is no good; for nineteenth-century industrial capitalism and our own more advanced technology have made it very difficult for "backward peoples" (to say noth-ing of ourselves in small units and groups) to make their living independently of somebody else nine thousand miles away. In other words we have destroyed the regional economies, and we offer a provincial remedy for the resulting evils; that is to say, a Utopian remedy which ignores our past experience. We guar-antee to the world freedom from fear. On this freedom I confess that I have nothing to say. Provincial arrogance could not go further; and if my own religion had not been destroyed by the same forces that destroyed Mr. Roosevelt's and Mr. Churchill's (I do not de-ny them or myself feelings of common piety), I should expect the wrath of God to strike them. I infer from the hedging cynicism of their repudiation of the Four Freedoms as an "offi-cial document" the casual frivolity with which they must have written it in the first place. There was a radio on the ship. The ease of modern communication compelled these gen-tlemen to communicate with the world, when there was nothing to communicate.

IV.   I am a little embarrassed at having used so many large con-ceptions, with so little specification. I ought to make plainer, before I go further, certain connections between regionalism and provincialism that I have only implied. The regional soci-ety is, with respect to high civilization, the neutral society: it can be primitive or highly cultivated, or any of the steps between. In the West our peculiar civilization was based upon regional autonomy, whose eccentricities were corrected and sublimated by the classical-Christian culture which provided a form for the highest development of man's potentialities *as man*. Man be-longed to his village, valley, mountain, or sea-coast; but wher-ever he was he was a Christian whose Hebraic discipline had tempered his tribal savagery and whose classical humanism had moderated the literal imperative of his Christianity to suicidal otherworldliness.

If this peculiar culture of the West is weakening or is even gone as a creative force, we are left with our diverse regionalisms; or *were* left with them. For the myth of science which undermined this culture and created the modern econo.nic man rooted out the regional economies, and is now creating a world regional economy. Regional economy means interdependence of the citizens of a region, whether the region be an Alpine village or the world. And the world, like the Alpine village, can be neutral with respect to high civilization. Regionalism without civilization—which means, with us, regionalism without the classical-Christian culture—becomes provincialism; and world regionalism becomes world provincialism. For provincialism is that state of mind in which regional men lose their origins in the past and its continuity into the present, and begin every day as if there had been no yesterday.

We are committed to this state of mind. We are so deeply involved in it (I make no exception of myself) that we must participate in its better purposes, however incomplete they may be; for good-will, even towards the Four Freedoms, is better than ill-will; and I am convinced that even the die-hard traditionalist would deny his own shrinking tradition if he refused to act for the remnant of it left because he can't have it all. For this remnant may be useful; there will be a minority with a memory which has not been dimmed by what Christian Gauss has called the Reversal of the Time Sense. We shall not all derive our standards of human nature and of the good society from an unexperienced future imagined by Mr. H. G. Wells or Mr. Henry Wallace.

V. EPILOGUE

The brilliant and unexpected renascence of Southern writing between the two wars is perhaps not of the first importance in the literature of the modern world; yet for the first time the South had a literature of considerable maturity which was distinctive enough to call for a special criticism which it failed to get. The provincial ideas of the critics of the North and East (there was no Southern criticism: merely a few Southern critics)—the provincial views of Southern writing of the recent renascence followed a direction somewhat as follows: The South, backward and illiberal, and controlled by white men who cherish a unique moral perversity, does not offer in itself a worthy subject to the novelist or the poet; it follows that the only acceptable literature that the South can produce must be a literature of social agitation, through which the need of reform may be publicized.

There were dozens of Southern novels written to this prescription. (I can think of only one Southern novelist of the period who ignored it and who was continuously popular: the late Elizabeth Madox Roberts.) The formula generally imposed two limitations upon the Southern writer: first, he must ignore the historical background of his subject; and second, he must judge the subject strictly in terms of the material welfare of his characters and of the "injustice" which keeps them from getting enough of it. My testimony is perhaps not wholly disinterested, yet I am convinced that not one distinguished novel was produced in or about the South from this point of view. The novel that came nearest to real distinction was probably Miss Glasgow's *Barren Ground*; but even this excellent novel is written outside the subject, with the result that the frustration of her Virginia farmers is not examined as an instance of the decay of rural culture everywhere, but rather as a simple object-lesson in the lack of standard American "advantages." (Miss Glasgow's other and later books pose other problems, chiefly the problem of the consciously "liberal" writer who draws his knowledge of human nature from a source richer than that of his ideas, and who thus writes somewhat below the level of his historical tradition.) But this is not a roster of all the sociological novels about the South from 1918 to the present. If these notes were a parlor game, I should challenge the "critics" who hailed them in the twenties and thirties to exhibit just one novel of this school which they would be willing to let compete with the best European writing of the period.

There has been some confusion in the South as well as elsewhere about the subjects accessible to Southern writers; this confusion results from the appeal to history: what *is* the structure of Southern society? What *was* it in the eighteen-forties and fifties? It is not necessary, fortunately, to answer those questions here. To bring these notes to a close I should like to make a few elementary distinctions. If the Southern subject is the destruction by war and the later degradation of the South by carpetbaggers and scalawags, and a consequent lack of moral force and imagination in the cynical materialism of the New South, then the sociologists of fiction and the so-called traditionalists are trying to talk about the same thing. But with this difference—and it is a difference between two worlds: the provincial world of the present, which sees in material welfare and legal justice the whole solution to the human problem; and the classical-Christian world, based upon the regional consciousness, which held that honor, truth, imagination, human dignity, and limited acquisitiveness, could alone justify a social order however rich and efficient it may be; and could do much to redeem an order dilapidated and corrupt, like the South today, if a few people passionately hold those beliefs.

So, in the period of the Southern renascence, our writers, poets as well as novelists, may be put into the two broad groups which I have indicated. Among the traditionalists whose work I believe will last I should name Stark Young, Elizabeth Madox Roberts, Katherine Anne Porter, Robert Penn Warren, Caroline Gordon, Ellen Glasgow (especially in *The Sheltered Life*), and William Faulkner, who is the most powerful and original novelist in the United States and one of the best in the modern world. It ought to be plain that by traditionalist I do not mean

E

a writer who either accepts or rejects the conventional picture of Southern life in the past. By the traditional as opposed to the provincial writer, I mean the writer who takes the South as he knows it today or can find out about it in the past, and who sees it as a region with some special characteristics, but otherwise offering as an imaginative subject the plight of human beings as it has been and will doubtless continue to be, here and in other parts of the world.

But if the provincial outlook, as I have glanced at it here, is to prevail, there is no reason to think that the South will remain immune to it. With the war of 1914-1918, the South re-entered the world—but gave a backward glance as it stepped over the border: that backward glance gave us the Southern renascence, a literature conscious of the past in the present. In the essay to which I referred in the first paragraph of these notes (I have now reread it) I said: "From the peculiarly historical consciousness of the Southern writer has come good work of a special order; but the focus of this consciousness is quite temporary. It has made possible the curious burst of intelligence that we get at a crossing of the ways, not unlike, on an infinitesimal scale, the outburst of poetic genius at the end of the sixteenth century when commercial England had already begun to crush feudal England." I see no reason to change that view.

From now on we are committed to seeing *with,* not *through* the eye: we, as provincials who do not live anywhere.

—1945

TECHNIQUES OF FICTION

THERE must be many techniques of fiction, but how many? I suppose a great many more than there are techniques of poetry. Why this should be so, if it is, nobody quite knows, and if we knew, I do not know what use the knowledge would have. For the great disadvantage of all literary criticism is its radical ignorance, which in the very nature of its aims must be incurable. Even the aims of criticism are unknown, beyond very short views; for example, in the criticism of the novel, Mr. Percy Lubbock tells us that the secret of the art is the strategy of "point of view"; Mr. E. M. Forster that the novelist must simply give us "life," or the illusion of "bouncing" us through it—which looks like a broader view than Mr. Lubbock's, until we pause to examine it, when it turns out to be worse than narrow, since to look at everything is to see nothing; or again Mr. Edwin Muir holds that "structure" is the key to the novelist's success or failure. There is no need here to explain what these critics mean by "point of view," or "life," or "structure"; but they all mean something useful—in a short view, beyond which (I repeat) critics seem to know little or nothing.

What the novelists know may be another thing altogether, and it is that knowledge which ought to be our deepest concern. You will have to allow me the paradox of presuming to know what the novelists know—or some of them at any rate—while as a critic I profess to know nothing. The presumption might encourage us to predict from the very nature of the critic's ignorance the nature and quality of the knowledge possible to good writers of fiction. The novelist keeps before him constantly the structure and substance of his fiction as a whole, to a degree to which the critic can never apprehend it. For the first cause of critical ignorance is, of course, the limitations of our minds, about which we can do little, work at them as we will. It is the special ignorance by which we, as critics, are limited in the act of reading any extended work of the imagination. The imagi-

native work must always differ to such a great degree as almost
to differ in kind from philosophical works, which our minds
apprehend and retain almost as wholes through the logical and
deductive structures which powerfully aid the memory. Who
can remember, well enough to pronounce upon it critically, all
of *War and Peace,* or *The Wings of the Dove,* or even *Death in Venice,*
the small enclosed world of which ought at least to do something to aid our memories? I have reread all three of these books
in the past year; yet for the life of me I could not pretend to know
them as wholes, and without that knowledge I lack the materials of criticism.

Because Mr. Lubbock seems to know more than anybody
else about this necessary ignorance of the critic, and for other
important reasons, I believe him to be the best critic who has
ever written about the novel. His book, *The Craft of Fiction,* is
very nearly a model of critical procedure. Even in so fine a study
as Albert Thibaudet's *Gustave Flaubert* there is nothing like the
actual, as opposed to the merely professed, critical modesty of
numerous statements like this by Lubbock: "Our critical fac-
ulty may be admirable; we may be thoroughly capable of judg-
ing a book justly, if only we could watch it at ease. But fine taste
and keen perception are of no use to us if we cannot retain the
image of the book; and the image escapes and evades us like a
cloud." Where, then, does Lubbock get the material of his criticism? He gets as much of it as any critic ever gets by means of
a bias which he constantly pushes in the direction of extreme
simplification of the novel in terms of "form," or "point of view"
(after James' more famous phrase, the "post of observation"),
or more generally in terms of the controlling intelligence which
determines the range and quality of the scene and the action. It
is the only book on fiction which has earned unanimous dislike
among other critics (I do not know three novelists who have
read it), and the reason, I think, is that it is, in its limited terms,
wholly successful; or, if that is too great praise, it is successful
in the same sense, and to no less degree than the famous lecture

notes on the Greek drama taken down by an anonymous student at the Lyceum in the fourth century B. C. The lecture notes
and *The Craft of Fiction* are studies of their respective arts in terms
of form; and I think that Lubbock had incomparably the more
difficult job to do. The novel has at no time enjoyed anything
like the number and the intensity of objective conventions which
the drama, even in its comparatively formless periods, has offered to the critic. The number of techniques possible in the
novel are probably as many as its conventions are few.

Having said so much in praise of Mr. Lubbock, I shall not,
I hope, seem to take it back if I say that even his intense awareness of what the novelist knows fails somehow, or perhaps inevitably, to get into his criticism. Anybody who has just read
his account of *Madame Bovary* comes away with a sense of loss,
which is the more intense if he has also just read that novel;
though what the loss is he no more than Mr. Lubbock will be
able to say. Yet no critic has ever turned so many different lights,
from so many different directions, upon any other novel (except
perhaps the lights that are called today the social and the historical); and yet what we get is not properly a revelation of the
techniques of *Madame Bovary* but rather what I should call a
marvellously astute chart of the operations of the central intelligence which binds all the little pieces of drama together into the
pictorial biography of a silly, sad, and hysterical little woman,
Emma Bovary. It is this single interest, this undeviating pursuit of one great clue, this sticking to the "short view" till the
last horn blows and night settles upon the hunting field, which
largely explains both the greatness of Mr. Lubbock's book and
the necessary and radical ignorance of criticism. We cannot be
both broad and critical, except in so far as knowledge of the
world, of ideas, and of man generally is broadening; but then
that knowledge has nothing to do specifically with the critical
job; it only keeps it from being inhuman. That is something;
but it is not criticism. To be critical is to be narrow in the crucial
act or process of judgment.

But after we gather up all the short views of good critics, and have set the limits to their various ignorances, we are confront-ed with what is left out or, if you will, left over: I have a strong suspicion that this residue of the novel or the story is what the author knew as he wrote it. It is what makes the little scenes, or even the big ones, "come off." And while we no doubt learn a 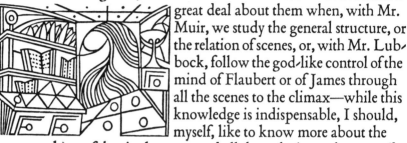 great deal about them when, with Mr. Muir, we study the general structure, or the relation of scenes, or, with Mr. Lub-bock, follow the god-like control of the mind of Flaubert or of James through all the scenes to the climax—while this knowledge is indispensable, I should, myself, like to know more about the making of the single scene, and all the techniques that contrib-ute to it; and I suspect that I am not asking the impossible, for this kind of knowledge is very likely the only kind that is actu-ally within our range. It alone can be got at, definitely and at par-ticular moments, even after we have failed, with Mr. Lubbock (honorable failure indeed), to "retain the image of the book."

It sounds very simple, as no doubt it is essentially a simple task to take a scene from a novel apart, and to see what makes it tick; but how to do it must baffle our best intentions. Suppose you want to understand by what arts Tolstoy, near the begin-ning of *War and Peace,* before the ground is laid, brings Peter, the bastard son of old Count Bezuhov, into the old Count's dying presence, and makes, of the atmosphere of the house and of the young man and the old man, both hitherto unknown to us, one of the great scenes of fiction: you would scarcely know better than I where to take hold of it, and I have only the merest clue. Suppose you feel, as I do, that after Rawdon Crawley comes home (I believe from gaol—it is hard to remember Thackeray) and finds Becky supping alone with Lord Steyne—suppose you feel that Thackeray should not have rung down the curtain the very moment Becky's exposure was achieved, but should have faced up to the tougher job of showing us Becky and Rawdon alone after Lord Steyne had departed: Is this a failure in a great novelist? If it is, why? The negative question, addressed to ourselves as persons interested in the techniques of an art, may also lead us to what the novelists know, or to much the same thing, what they should have known. And, to come nearer home, what is the matter with Ty Ty Walden's philosophical meditations, towards the end of *God's Little Acre,* which freezes up our credulity and provokes our fiercest denial? It is surely not that Ty Ty is merely expressing as well as he can the doctrine of the innate goodness of man in the midst of depravity. That doctrine will do as well as any other in the mouth of a fictional character provided his scene and his experience within the scene entitle him to utter it; but before we can believe that Ty Ty is actually thinking anything whatever, we have got in the first place to believe that Ty Ty is a man—which is precisely what Mr. Caldwell evidently did not think it important to make us do.

How shall we learn what to say about particular effects of the story, without which the great over-all structure and movement of the human experience which is the entire novel cannot be made credible to us? The professional critics pause only at intervals to descend to these minor effects which are of course the problems without which the other, more portentous problems which engage criticism could not exist. The fine artists of fiction, I repeat, because they produce these effects must understand them. And having produced them, they are silent about the ways they took to produce them, or paradoxical and mysterious like Flaubert, who told Maupassant to go to the station and look at the cab drivers until he understood the typical cab driver, and then to find the language to distinguish one cab driver from all others in the world. It is the sort of *obiter dicta* which can found schools and movements, and the schools and movements often come to some good, even though the slogan, like this one, means little.

I suppose only the better novelists, like Defoe, Madame de

La Fayette, Turgeniev, Dickens, Flaubert, many others as great as these, some greater, like Tolstoy and Dostoevsky, knew the special secrets which I am trying, outside criticism, so to speak, to bring before you. There is almost a masonic tradition in the rise of any major art, from its undifferentiated social beginnings to the conscious aptitude which is the sign of a developed art form. Doubtless I ought to repeat once more that for some reason the moment the secrets of this aptitude come within the *provenance* of formal criticism, they vanish. They survive in the works themselves, and in the living confraternity of men of letters, who pass on by personal instruction to their successors the "tricks of the trade." The only man I have known in some twenty years of literary experience who was at once a great novelist and a great teacher, in this special sense, was the late Ford Madox Ford. His influence was immense, even upon writers who did not know him, even upon other writers, today, who have not read him. For it was through him more than any other man writing in English in our time that the great traditions of the novel came down to us. Joyce, a greater writer than Ford, represents by comparison a more restricted practice of the same literary tradition, a tradition that goes back to Stendhal in France and to Jane Austen in England, coming down to us through Flaubert, James, Conrad, Joyce, Virginia Woolf and Ernest Hemingway.

It is a tradition which has its own secrets to offer; yet in saying that I am not claiming for it greater novelists than some other school can produce or novelists greater than those who just happen. There is Meredith (for those who, like Ramon Fernandez, can read him); there is Thomas Hardy, there is even the early H. G. Wells. But there is not Arnold Bennett; there is not Mr. Galsworthy; not Hugh Walpole nor Frank Swinnerton. This is prejudice, not criticism. And these are all Britons, not Americans. I have no desire to play 'possum on the American question. Yet I am convinced that among American novelists who have had large publics since the last war, only Dreiser, Faulkner, and Hemingway are of major importance. There are "good" popular novelists who have done much to make us at home physically in our own country; they have given us our scenes, our people, and above all our history; and these were necessary to the preliminary knowledge of ourselves which we have been a little late in getting and which must be got and assimilated if we are going to be a mature people. Possibly the American novel had to accomplish the task that in Europe had been done by primitive chronicle, mémoire, ballad, strolling player. The American novel has had to find a new experience, and only in our time has it been able to pause for the difficult task of finding out how to get itself written. That is an old story with us, yet beneath it lies a complexity of feeling that from Hawthorne down to our time has baffled our best understanding. The illus⁄ tration is infinite in its variety. At this moment I think of my two favorite historians, Herodotus and Joinville, and I am em⁄ barrassed from time to time because Herodotus, the pagan, seems nearer to my experience than Joinville, the Christian chronicler of St. Louis. It is perhaps easier for us to feel comfortable with the remote and relatively neutral elements of our culture. Those experiences of Europe which just precede or overlap the Amer⁄ ican experience bemuse us, and introduce a sort of chemical ambivalence into our judgment. Joinville is both nearer to me than Herodotus, and less immediate. What American could not be brought to confess a similar paradox? To our Europ⁄ ean friends who are now beginning to know us, and who in all innocence may subscribe to the popular convention of The Simple American Mind, I would say, if it is not too impolite: Beware.

But the American novel is not my present subject, nor, thank heaven, the American mind. My subject is merely the technique of fiction which now at last I feel that I am ready to talk about, not critically, you understand, but as a member of a guild. Ford used to say that he wrote his novels in the tone of one English gentleman whispering into the ear of another English gentle⁄

man: how much irony he intended I never knew; I hope a great deal. I intend none at all when I say that these remarks are set down by an artisan for other artisans.

Gustave Flaubert created the modern novel. Gustave Flaubert created the modern short story. He created both because he created modern fiction. I am not prepared to say that he created all our fictional forms and structures, the phases of the art of fiction that interest Mr. Lubbock and Mr. Muir. He did not originate all those features of the short story which interest historians and anthologists. These are other matters altogether. And I do not like to think that Flaubert created modern fiction because I do not like Flaubert. It was the fashion in France, I believe, until the Fall, to put Stendhal above Flaubert. I am not sure but I suspect that a very tired generation felt more at ease with a great writer whose typical heroes are persons of mere energy and whose books achieve whatever clarity and form that they do achieve as an accident of the moral ferocity of the author. But without *Le Rouge et Le Noir,* or without what it put into circulation in French literary *milieu* after 1830, Flaubert could not have written *Madame Bovary.* I do not like to think that Stendhal did this because I do not like Stendhal. Both Stendhal and Flaubert had the single dedication to art which makes the disagreeable man. Doubtless it would be pleasanter if the great literary discoveries could be made by gentlemen like Henry James, who did make his share, and who, of course, was a greater novelist than either of these Frenchmen; or by English squires; but we have got to take them, as Henry James would not do in the instance of Flaubert, as they come, and they often come a little rough.

A moment ago I introduced certain aspersions upon a few English novelists of the recent past, but it was with a purpose, for their limitations, sharply perceived by the late Virginia Woolf in her famous essay *Mr. Bennett and Mrs. Brown,* will make quite clear the difference between the novelist who, with Mr. Forster, merely bounces us along and the novelist who tries to do the whole job, the job that Flaubert first taught him to do. Mrs. Woolf is discussing Hilda Lessways, Arnold Bennett's heroine, and she says:

> *But we cannot hear her mother's voice, or Hilda's voice; we can only hear Mr. Bennett's voice telling us facts about rents and free-holds and copyholds and fines. What can Mr. Bennett be about? I have formed my own opinion of what Mr. Bennett is about—he is trying to make us imagine for him.* . . .

"Trying to make us imagine for him" —the phrase erects a Chinese wall between all that is easy, pleas-ant, and perhaps merely socially useful in modern fiction, and all that is rigorous, sober, and self-contained. Mrs. Woolf, again, in speaking of the novels of Galsworthy, Bennett and Wells, says:

> *Yet what odd books they are! Sometimes I wonder if we are right to call them books at all. For they leave one with a strange feeling of incom-pleteness and dissatisfaction. In order to complete them it seems necessary to do something—to join a society, or, more desperately, to write a cheque.*

That is very nearly the whole story: the novelist who tries to make us im-agine for him is perhaps trying to make us write a cheque—a very good thing to do, and I am not sure that even the socially unconscious Flaubert was deeply opposed to it, though I shall not attempt to speak for him on the question of joining societies. Let us see this matter as reasonably as we can. All literature has a social or moral or religious purpose: the writer has something that he has got to say to the largest public possible. In spite of Flaubert's belief that he wrote only for himself, this is as true of *Madame Bovary* as of *Uncle Tom's Cabin*. Is there a real difference between these books that might justify us in setting apart two orders of literature? Perhaps; for the difference is very great be-tween getting it all inside the book and leaving some of it irre-

sponsibly outside. For even though the cheque be written in a
good cause it is the result of an irresponsible demand upon the
part of the novelist. But the distinction is not, I think, absolute,
nor should it be. And I am sure that Sainte-Beuve was right
when he wrote in his review of *Madame Bovary* that not all young
married women in Normandy were like Emma: was there not
the case of the childless young matron of central France who,
instead of taking lovers and then taking arsenic, "adopted children about her . . . and instructed them in moral culture"? Very
good; for it is obvious that persons who join societies and write
cheques for moral culture are proper characters of fiction, as
indeed all human beings of all degrees of charity or misanthropy
are. But that is not the point at issue.

That point is quite simply that Flaubert, for the first time
consciously and systematically, but not for the first time in the
history of fiction, and not certainly of poetry—Flaubert taught
us how to put this overworked and allegorical cheque *into* the
novel, into its complex texture of scene, character and action:
which, of course, is one way of saying that he did the complete
imaginative job himself, and did not merely point to what was
going on, leaving the imaginative specification to our good will
or to our intellectual vanity. (I pause here to remark the existence of a perpetual type of critic who prefers inferior literature,
because it permits him to complete it. Flaubert understood the
critics who, committed to the public function of teacher, resent
being taught.) This completeness of presentation in the art of
fiction was not, I repeat, something new, but I gather that it had
previously appeared only here and there, by the sheer accident
of genius: I think of Petronius; a few incidents in Boccaccio;
half a dozen scenes by the Duke of Saint-Simon (the memor-
ialists shade imperceptibly into the novelists); the great scene in
which the Prince de Clèves tells his wife that he has refrained
from expressing his love for her because he wished to avoid
conduct improper to a husband; Emma Woodhouse with
Mr. Knightly at the parlor table looking at the picture-album;

countless other moments in early prose literature; but most of all that great forerunner, *Moll Flanders,* which is so much all of a piece in the Flaubertian canon that sometimes I think that Flaubert wrote it; or that nobody wrote either Defoe or Flaubert. For when literature reaches this stage of maturity, it is anony-mous, and it matters little who writes it.

This is extravagant language. Or is it? It is no more than we are accustomed to when we talk about poetry, or music, or most of all the classical drama. The fourth-century lecture notes, to which I have already referred, some time ago licensed the most pretentious claims for the stage, and for poetry generally. I am only saying that fiction can be, has been, and *is* an art, as the various poetries are arts. Is this an extravagant claim? Only, I am convinced, in the minds of the more relaxed practitioners of this art, who excuse something less than the utmost talent and effort, and in the minds of critics who find the critical task no more exacting than historical reporting, which reduces the novel to a news supplement. Was, as a matter of fact, Emma typical of young Norman womanhood? Are the Okies and Arkies just as Steinbeck represents them? What a triumph for the historians when it was found that there had actually been a young man whose end was like Julien Sorel's! And is it true what Mr. William Faulkner says about Dixie? If it is, is what Mr. Stark Young says also true? This, I submit, is the temper of American criticism of fiction, with rare exceptions of little influence.

> *Was it for this the wild geese spread*
> *The grey wing upon every tide;*
> *For this that all that blood was shed,*
> *For this that Edward Fitzgerald died,*
> *And Robert Emmet and Wolfe Tone,*
> *All that delirium of the brave?*

If you will substitute for these Irish heroes the heroes of the modern novel, Flaubert, Dostoevsky, James, Joyce, you will see through the wrong end of the telescope the present condition of criticism of the novel in the narrowing perspective of decay.

It is time now, towards the end of this *causerie,* to produce an image, an *exemplum,* something out of the art of fiction that underlies all the major problems of "picture and drama," symmetry, foreshortening, narrative pattern, pace and language—all those complexities of the novelist's art which Henry James, alone of the great fictionists, tried to explain (how much he coyly evaded!) in his famous Prefaces: problems that laid the ground for Mr. Lubbock's beautiful study. I am looking for something very simple and, in its direct impact, conclusive; a scene or an incident that achieves fulness of realization in terms of what it gives us to see and to hear. It must offer us fulness of rendition, not mere direction or statement. Don't state, says James, time and again—render! Don't tell us what is happening, let it happen! So I would translate James. For our purposes here it cannot be too great a scene, if we would see all round it: it must be a scene that will give us the most elementary instruction in that branch of the art of which the critics tell us little. What shall it be? Shall it be Prince André lying wounded under the wide heavens? Shall it be Moll Flanders peeping out of the upstairs window of the inn at her vanishing fourth (or is it fifth?) and undivorced husband, slyly avoiding him because she is in the room with her fifth or is it sixth? I could find perfect *exempla* in James himself. What could be better than Milly Theale's last soirée before she becomes too ill to appear again? Then there are James' fine "sittingroom scenes," the man and the woman talking out the destiny of one or both of them: Lambert Strether and Maria Gostrey, John Marcher and May Bartram, Merton Densher and Milly Theale. Or there is Strether looking down upon the boat in which Chad Newsome and Madame de Vionnet, unaware of Strether's scrutiny, betray that air of intimacy which discloses them for the first time to Strether as lovers.

Yet about these excellent scenes there is something outside our purpose, a clue that would sidetrack us into the terms of form and structure which I have virtually promised to neglect. Let us select an easy and perhaps even quite vulgar scene, a stock scene, in fact, that we should expect to find in a common romantic novel, or even in a Gothic story provided the setting were re‑ duced to the bourgeois scale. Let the situation be something like this: A pretty young married woman, bored with her husband, a small‑town doctor, has had an affair of sentiment with a young man, who has by this time left town. Growing more desperate, she permits herself to be seduced by a neighboring landowner, a coarse Lothario, who soon tires of her. Our scene opens with the receipt of his letter of desertion. He is going away and will not see her again. The young woman receives the letter with agitation and runs upstairs to the attic, where having read the letter she gives way to hysteria. She looks out the window down into the street, and decides to jump and end it all. But she grows dizzy and recoils. After a moment she hears her husband's voice; the servant touches her arm; she comes to and recovers.

It is distinctly unpromising: James would not have touched it; Balzac, going the whole hog, might have let her jump, or perhaps left her poised for the jump while he resumed the ad‑ ventures of Vautrin. But in any case there she stands, and as I have reported the scene you have got to take my word for it that she is there at all: you do not see her, you do not hear the rapid breathing and the beating heart, and you have, again, only my word for it that she is dizzy. What I have done here, in fact, is precisely what Mrs. Woolf accused the Georgian novelists of doing: I am trying to make you imagine for me, perhaps even covertly trying to make you write a cheque for the Society for the Improvement of Provincial Culture, or the Society for the Relief of Small Town Boredom, or for a subscription to the Book of the Month Club which would no doubt keep the young woman at improving her mind, and her mind off undesirable lovers. I hope that we shall do all these good things. But you must bear in mind that the Book of the Month Club would probably send her the kind of literature that I have just written for you, so that she too might take to writing cheques. Is there any guarantee that they would be good cheques? The question brings us up short against certain permanent disabilities of human nature, which we should do well to see as objectively as possible, in the language of a greater artist; which is just what we shall now proceed to do:

Charles was there; she saw him; he spoke to her; she heard nothing, and she went on quickly up the stairs, breathless, distraught, dumb, and ever holding this horrible piece of paper, that crackled between her fingers like a plate of sheet-iron. On the second floor she stopped before the attic door, that was closed.

Then she tried to calm herself; she recalled the letter; she must finish it; she did not dare to. And where? How? She would be seen! "Ah, no! here," she thought, "I shall be all right."

Emma pushed open the door and went in.

The slates threw straight down a heavy heat that gripped her temples, stifled her; she dragged herself to the closed garret-window. She drew back the bolt, and the dazzling light burst in with a leap.

Opposite, beyond the roofs, stretched the open country till it was lost to sight. Down below, underneath her, the village square was empty; the stones of the pavement glittered, the weathercocks on the houses were motionless. At the corner of the street, from a lower story, rose a kind of humming with strident modulations. It was Binet turning.

She leant against the embrasure of the window, and reread the letter with angry sneers. But the more she fixed her attention upon it, the more confused were her ideas. She saw him again, heard him, encircled him with her arms, and the throbs of her heart, that beat against her breast like blows of a sledge-hammer, grew faster and faster, with uneven intervals. She looked about her with the wish that the earth might crumble into pieces. Why not end it all? What restrained her? She was free. She advanced, looked at the paving-stones, saying to herself, "Come! Come!"

The luminous ray that came straight up from below drew the weight of her body towards the abyss. It seemed to her that the ground of the oscillating square went up the walls, and that the floor dipped on end like a tossing boat. She was right at the edge, almost hanging, surrounded by vast space. The blue of the heavens suffused her, the air was whirling in her hollow head; she had but to yield, to let herself be taken; and the humming of the lathe never ceased, like an angry voice calling her.

"Emma! Emma!" cried Charles.

She stopped.

"Wherever are you? Come!"

The thought that she had just escaped from death made her almost faint with terror. She closed her eyes; then she shivered at the touch of a hand on her sleeve; it was Félicité.

"Master is waiting for you, madame; the soup is on the table."

And she had to go down to sit at table.

The English translation is not good; its failure to convey the very slight elevation of tone is a fundamental failure. It is not a rhetorical elevation, but rather one of perfect formality and sobriety. We are not looking at this scene through Emma's eyes. We occupy a position slightly above and to one side, where we see her against the full setting; yet observe how at the same time we see nothing that she does not see, hear nothing that she does not hear. It is one of the amazing paradoxes of the modern novel, whose great subject is a man alone in society or even against society, almost never with society, that out of this view of man isolated we see developed to the highest possible point of virtuosity and power a technique of putting man wholly into his physical setting. The action is not stated from the point of view of the author; it is rendered in terms of situation and scene. To have made this the viable property of the art of fiction was to have virtually made the art of fiction. And that, I think, is our debt to Flaubert.

But we should linger over this scene if only to try our hands at what I shall now, for the first time, call sub-criticism, or the animal tact which permits us occasionally to see connections and correspondences which our rational powers, unaided, cannot detect. What capital feature of the scene seems (if it does) to render the actuality more than any other? The great fact, I think, is the actuality, and your sense of it is all that is necessary. Yet I like to linger over the whirring lathe of old Binet, a lay figure or "flat character" who has done little in the novel and will never do much, and whose lathe we merely noted from the beginning as a common feature of a small town like Yonville. I should like to know when Flaubert gave him the lathe, whether just to tag him for us; whether, writing the present scene, he went back and gave it to him as a "plant" for use here later; or whether, having given him the lathe, he decided it would be useful in this scene.

What is its use? James said that the work of fiction must be "a direct impression of life," a very general requirement; but in the perspective of nearly ninety years since the publication of *Madame Bovary* and the rise of the Impressionist novel through Henry James, James Joyce, and Virginia Woolf, the phrase takes on a more specific sense. Mind you the phrase is not "direct representation," which only the stage can give us. But here, using this mechanic's tool, Flaubert gives us a direct *impression* of Emma's sensation at a particular moment (which not even the drama could accomplish), and thus by rendering audible to us what Emma alone could hear he charged the entire scene with actuality. As Emma goes to the window she merely notes that Binet's lathe is turning—*C'était Binet qui tournait.* Then she looks down at the street which seems to rise towards her—*Allons! Allons!* she whispers, because she cannot find the will to jump. We have had rendered to us visually the shock of violent suicide. Now comes the subtle fusion of the reaction and of the pull toward self-destruction, which is the humming in her head: how can Flaubert *render* it for us? Shall we not have to take his word for it? Shall we not have to imagine for him? No: *l'air circulait dans sa tête creuse,* he says; and then: *le ronflement du tour ne discontinuait pas, comme une voix furieuse qui l'appelait*—"the whir-

ring of the lathe never stopped like a voice of fury calling her."
The humming vertigo that draws the street towards her is rendered audible to us by the correlative sound of the lathe.

That is all, or nearly all, there is to it; but I think it is enough
to set up our image, our *exemplum*. I leave to you, as I constantly
reserve for myself, the inexhaustible pleasure of tracing out the
infinite strands of interconnection in this and other novels, complexities as deep as life itself but ordered, fixed, and dramatized
into arrested action. If I have made too much of Flaubert, or
too much of too little of Flaubert, I can only say that I have not
wilfully ignored men as great, or greater. It is proper to honor
France, and to honor the *trouvère,* the discoverer; for it has been
through Flaubert that the novel has at last caught up with poetry.

—1944

A READING OF KEATS

IT IS proper that we celebrate the hundred and fiftieth anniversary of the birth of John Keats by testing our powers of reading him. For the perpetual task of criticism, every generation or
two, is to understand again the poetry of the past. Poetry which
cannot survive this renewal of understanding, and live again
in the critical sensibility of posterity, must contain some radical
flaw of interest; it is perhaps in this sense that time is the test of
poetry. This view, commonly held today, presupposes the continuity of tradition which with occasional lapses has come down
to us from the Greeks; but whether the best English poets shall
survive the coming age is a question bearing less upon their
value for us than upon our capacity to receive it. If Keats goes
unread by the next generation, whose memory will not go back
to the great historical era which now seems to be closing, I cannot think that the failure will be his. He will remain one of the
great English poets for a later generation to rediscover.

This sounds like the prediction of Colvin in 1917; and I see
no reason to argue generally with the Victorian estimate. Perhaps of Keats alone of the English romantics does this estimate
still hold, possibly because the great claims were never made for
him that were made for Wordsworth and Coleridge. If definitive criticism were possible, Bridges's *A Critical Introduction to
Keats* (1894, revised 1914) and A. C. Bradley's "The Letters of
Keats" (*Oxford Lectures on Poetry*, 1909) might be said to realise
it; and to these should be added the fine textual study, Professor Ridley's *Keats' Craftsmanship* (1933), and Professor C. D.
Thorpe's *The Mind of John Keats* (1926). (The value of Professor Thorpe's book is somewhat diminished by the instability of
his critical terms; but as a rounded descriptive study it is excellent. I have not put Mr. Murry's *Keats and Shakespeare* [1926] in
this list because I find its main argument incomprehensible;
though the book is valuable for many brilliant insights.) So,
apart from the three full-length biographies by Houghton, Col-

vin, and Miss Lowell, there are four excellent critical studies
of Keats, two from the late Victorian age, two from our own:
there is probably less useless writing about Keats than about the
other great English romantics. The reasons for this are obvious
if a little hard to state: the bulk of Keats's work is comparatively
slight; at his best (the odes, "Lamia," "The Eve of St. Agnes,"
and parts of "Hyperion") he has a masterful simplicity of purpose and control; in these poems, with the single exception of
"Hyperion," the influences are so well assimilated that only
the most trivial academic mind could suppose Keats's relation
to the "history of ideas" to have more than the value of a few
monographs. In this I take it "he is with Shakespeare." It has
been easier for the critics to get at the essentials of Keats than of
Wordsworth, Coleridge, and Shelley, who conceal more traps
to catch scholars.

This is not to say that Keats was, in the sense of the phrase
common a few years ago, a "pure poet." He was the great poet
of his age, in the fullest sense; and even Matthew Arnold almost
let himself see that he was. Arnold's essay remains one of the
best "estimates" of Keats in the Victorian style (which goes back
to Johnson) of combined moral and critical judgment; perhaps
Arnold was the last great critic to use it effectively; for since its
decay in the impressionism of Pater and in the dilettanteism of
the "literary essay" of the nineties and early nineteen-hundreds,
we have been getting a new sort of criticism which was brought
in by Eliot's *The Sacred Wood* (1920).

Arnold's essay still has a certain interest in the history of
Keats's reputation, yet it must interest us now as perhaps the best
evidence of Arnold's almost perverse use of critical standards.
More than any other poet Keats pinned him upon the horns of
his dilemma: "Natural magic" and/or "Moral interpretation."
It has been said (by whom I do not remember) that the ambig-
uousness of Arnold's judgment of Keats was due to his hu-
morless sense of responsibility for the poetry of his age: Keats
was the greatest "natural magician" since Shakespeare; but what

poetry then *needed* was moral interpretation, and Keats had been a harmful example. This is not the place to examine Arnold's critical dialectic (that has been admirably done by Mr. Trilling); yet it is not beside the point to remark Arnold's failure to see that in Keats's "principle of beauty in all things" lay a possible way out of his dilemma. Even the *Letters* (among the great letters of the world) give a clue to its significance, to say nothing of the structure of the odes. Arnold was not interested in structure unless it was a structure of action inviting moral interpretation. He saw Keats quite simply as a "sensuous" poet.

I have belabored this question more than either Arnold or it deserves (not more than they merit) because I think it is necessary, before proceeding to Keats's poetry, to refer briefly to my own disabilities as a critic of Keats. They are not unlike Arnold's. It would be ludicrous to confess that I lack Arnold's general powers, or more particularly his capacity for awareness of what he did not like (it was this awareness that raised him above the level of the conventional Victorian moralist); but it is not beside the point to warn readers of this essay that my attitude towards Keats is reverent, yet distant without disinterestedness. Whether Keats is what we *need* I do not know; yet we neither want him nor use him. For the past fifteen years the direction of Anglo-American poetry has been rather towards Shelley than Keats, towards "Godwin-perfectibility" and social consciousness than towards a dramatic-symbolic style. I hope I shall not sound like Margaret Fuller if I say that I am not indifferent to the utmost capacity of men for social and individual perfection; I simply do not think that poetry should be limited to exhorting men to these goods. My lack of sympathy with this school nevertheless does not qualify me as a critic of Keats, in spite of my conviction (which was Arnold's unhappy conviction) that Keats was in one of the great modes of poetry. It is perhaps a mode inaccessible to us today. I shall not try, because it is too difficult, to state directly why I think this obstacle exists; my understanding of it, such as it may be, will be implied in what I am about to say of "Ode to a Nightingale," in my opinion Keats's great poem in spite of its imperfect detail, greater than "Ode to Autumn," which because of its purity of tone and style Bridges ranks first among the odes; "Ode to Autumn" is a very nearly perfect piece of style but it has little to say. Because I believe that "Ode to a Nightingale" at least tries to say everything that poetry can say I am putting it at the centre of this discussion.

II.   The testimony of the criticism of Keats which I have read (I cannot pause to summarise it here) is that he was a pictorial poet in the Spenserian tradition. I would add to this very general statement the observation: his progress from "Endymion" to the revised "Hyperion" is a direct line, at the end of which he achieved under Milton's influence a new kind of blank verse; but in it he could not control the heroic action. In a letter to Reynolds (September 21st, 1819), he said: "I have given up 'Hyperion'—there were too many Miltonic inversions in it . . ."; and in a letter to George Keats, written six days later: "I have but lately stood on my guard against Milton. Life to him would be death to me." I think the second of these explanations, general as it is, comes nearer to the truth: he could not write Miltonic verse without eventual frustration because he lacked a Miltonic subject; it would be "death" to him. For the framework of "Hyperion," of the more human, revised version no less than of the first version, is pictorial, with declamatory summaries of action which Keats does not present. It is a succession of plastic scenes.

If this had been the only line of development from "Endymion," we should not, of course, have got the odes; and Keats would have remained a youthful experimenter of genius, considerably above Chatterton but not so impressive as Shelley. The other line runs in the order of time, from "Endymion" to the odes; but perhaps technically, as Professor Ridley has argued, the line is from the sonnets to the odes; that is to say, his experiments with the sonnet led him to modifications of the form which gave us the great stanzas of the Grecian Urn and the Nightingale. And within that narrow, lyrical, and potentially dramatic compass he had something ready to say that he could not have said in the other kinds of verse that he had tried. "The Eve of St. Agnes" is his masterpiece in the Spenserian tradition of *ut pictura, poesis,* and the originality is in the freshness of the language. Far more instructive for technical reasons (reasons which cannot be disconnected from the higher reasons) is the versification of "Lamia," based partly upon Dryden, but, as Professor Ridley shows, in no sense imitative. For example, "Lamia" has proportionately three times as many run-on lines as Dryden's *Fables* taken as a whole, thirty-three per cent being run on; there is a large number of tercets ending with alexandrines; but there are no feminine endings. The result of this adaptation of Dryden's verse is a movement of great speed and flexibility, firm yet supple; and altogether the most original contribution to narrative verse of the nineteenth century. But it should be remembered that "Lamia" is a narrative of a minor mythological incident which Keats picked up in Burton, not epic action: although Keats failed to sustain his blank verse because he could not fill it with action, he succeeded brilliantly with a new kind of verse in which the pictorial method supports the main effect, the simple action turning on a plot of recognition. For the moment we need not go into the symbolism; but it is significant that it was material which Keats found something like the perfect means to bring into form. Written in the summer of 1819 (Part I by mid-July), "Lamia" is the height of his achievement in the long poem. The important thing to remember is that Keats finished it at about the same time that he abandoned "Hyperion."

I shall briefly anticipate the end that I am heading towards by setting down a few opinions which will both indicate its direction and gauge my understanding of Keats. "Lamia" is more closely related to the two great odes, the Nightingale and the Grecian Urn, than to "Hyperion," and the fact that he could successfully revise "The Eve of St. Agnes" at the time he was finishing "Lamia" is as much proof as criticism needs that it is not too far from the materials and methods of a poem which some critics would put with the other narratives, "Isabella" and the fragment "The Eve of St. Mark." Moreover, we must think of "Lamia" and "The Eve of St. Agnes" along with the great odes, as follows: "Ode to a Nightingale," "Ode on a Grecian Urn," "Ode to Psyche," "To Autumn," and "Ode on Melancholy." This cluster of poems is the centre of Keats's great work, and they all deal with the same imaginative dilemma—or, if we wish to be biographical, the same conflict in Keats's experience. (I cannot agree with Bridges that there is anything in the sonnets as good as the best Shakespeare; I am convinced that they would not have won their great reputation apart from the other work; and I shall not discuss them here.)

The imaginative dilemma of Keats is, I assume, implicit in the poems, which are at its best statement: the most that criticism ought to attempt is perhaps a kind of circulatory description of its movements, from poem to poem. Bridges's astute remark that "Keats's art is primarily objective and pictorial, and whatever other qualities it has are as it were *added on to things as perceived*," contains critical insight of the first order. I have italicized *added on to things as perceived*, and I would double the italics of the last two words; they point directly to the imaginative limit of Keats's poetry, one horn of the dilemma out of which it does not move, in which it must, if it is to exceed the *ut pictura, poesis* formula, seek some conversion of that limit.

I should thus offer (for what it is worth) the very general analysis: Keats as a pictorial poet was necessarily presenting in a given poem a series of scenes, and even in the narratives the action does not flow from inside the characters, but is governed pictorially from the outside. He is thus a painting poet and would have earned Lessing's censure. But like every great artist

H

he knew (in his own terms, which are none of our business) that his problem was to work within his limitations, and to transcend them. He was a poet of space whose problem was to find a way of conveying what happens in time; for it is time in which dramatic conflict takes place; and it is only by conver⁄ sion into dramatic actuality that the parts of the verbal painting achieve relation and significance. "The form of thought in Keats," says Mr. Kenneth Burke, "is mystical, in terms of an eternal present"—and, I should add, in terms of the arrested action of painting.

III. When Keats adds to "things as perceived," what does he add? That, it seems to me, is the special problem of Keats. In the simplest language it is the problem of adding movement to a static picture, of putting into motion the "languor which lingers in the main design" (Bridges) of even the later work.

Of the eight stanzas of "Ode to a Nightingale" six are distinct⁄ ly pictorial in method; a seventh, stanza three, in which Keats expresses his complaint of common life, develops as a medita⁄ tion out of the second stanza, the picture of Provence. The only stanza which does not give us or in some way pertain to a definite scene is number seven; for though the method there is pictorial, the effect is allusive: the permanence of the nightingale's song is established in a rapid series of vignettes, ending with the famous "faëry lands forlorn." It is the only stanza, as some critic has remarked, which contains a statement contradictory of our sense of common reality.

Thou wast not born for death, immortal Bird,
he

says to the nightingale; and we cannot agree. The assertion is out of form in an obvious sense; for the poem is an accumulation of pictorial situations; and the claim of immortality for the bird is dramatic and lyrical.

I am raising the question whether the metonymy which at⁄ tributes to the literal nightingale the asserted immortality of the song is convincing enough to carry the whole imaginative insight of the poem. I think it is, given the limits of Keats's art, but I am still nagged by a difficulty that will not down. It seems to me that the ambivalence of the nightingale symbol contains almost the whole substance of the poem: the bird, as bird, shares the mortality of the world; as symbol, it purports to transcend it. And I feel that the pictorial technique has not been quite dramatic enough to give to the transcendence of the symbol life in some visibly presented experience. The far more implausible, even far-fetched, metaphor of the draughtsman's compasses, in Donne, comes out a little better because through a series of dialectical transformations, from the dying man to the Ptolemaic spheres, and then through the malleable gold to the compasses, there is a progression of connected analogies, given us step by step; and we acknowledge the identity of compasses and lovers as imaginatively possible. Keats merely *asserts*: song equals immortality; and I feel there is some disparity between the symbol and what it is expected to convey—not an inherent disparity, for such is not imaginatively conceivable; but a disparity such as we should get in the simple equation $A = B$, if we found that the assigned values of A and B were respectively 1 and 3.

This feature of Keats's art we shall find in "Ode on a Grecian Urn" but not in "Ode to Psyche." I confess that I do not know what to do about this anomalous poem, except to admire it. There appears to me to be very little genuine *sensation* in Keats (rather what Arnold and his contemporaries mistook for sensation), but there is more of it in "Ode to Psyche" than anywhere else in the great odes. Mr. T. S. Eliot puts it first among the great odes, possibly because most of its detail is genuinely experienced and because it contains no developed attitude towards life. The other odes do; and it is an attitude less mature than that which Mr. Eliot finds in the *Letters*. With this part of his view of Keats one must agree. But it is a dangerous view, since it is very remotely possible that some letters from Shakespeare may turn up some day. But Mr. Eliot's preference for "Ode to

Psyche" doubtless shares at bottom the common prejudice that romantic art tends not only to be pictorial but "off centre" and lacking in that appearance of logical structure which we ordinarily associate with Donne and Dryden. I do not want to get into this classical-and-romantic affair, for the usual reason, and for a reason of my own, which is that it has a way of backfiring. Mr. Eliot has said that Coleridge and Wordsworth on one side are "as eighteenth century as anybody." So is Keats. The apostrophe to the nightingale, which I have been at some pains to try to understand, is quite "eighteenth century"; but it is not nearly so eighteenth century as the entire third stanza, which I shall now try to understand, assuming that what it says has a close connection with that literal part of the nightingale, the physical bird, which Keats seems not to know what to do with (except to make it, in the last stanza, fly away). Here it is:

> *Fade far away, dissolve, and quite forget*
> *What thou among the leaves hast never known,*
> *The weariness, the fever, and the fret*
> *Here where men sit and hear each other groan;*
> *Where palsy shakes a few, sad, last gray hairs,*
> *Where youth grows pale, and spectre-thin, and dies;*
> *Where but to think is to be full of sorrow*
> *And leaden-eyed despairs,*
> *Where beauty cannot keep her lustrous eyes,*
> *Or new Love pine at them beyond tomorrow.**

*Quotations from the poems follow Garrod, The Poetical Works of John Keats (Oxford, 1939).

§ Sidney Colvin, John Keats (New York, 1917), p. 419.

Looked at from any point of view, this stanza is bad; the best that one ought to say of it perhaps is that there are worse things in Shelley and Wordsworth, and in Keats himself. (Even Colvin's habitual tone of eulogy is restrained when he comes to it.§) It is bad in the same way as the passages in Shelley's "Adonaïs" which exhibit the troops of mourners are bad. Keats here is relapsing into weakened eighteenth-century rhetoric; Blake could have put into the personifications imaginative power, and Pope genuine feeling, or at any rate an elegance and vigor which would have carried them.

There is not space enough in an essay to go into this matter as it needs to be gone into. What I wish to indicate, for the consideration of more thorough readers, is that stanza three may be of the utmost significance in any attempt to understand the structure of Keats's poetry. It gives us a "picture" of common reality, in which the life of man is all mutability and frustration. But here if anywhere in the poem the necessity to dramatize time, or the pressure of actuality, is paramount. *Keats has no language of his own for this realm of experience.* That is the capital point. He either falls into the poetic language of the preceding age, or, if he writes spontaneously, he commits his notorious errors of taste; in either case the language is not adequate to the feeling; or, to put it "cognitively," he lacks an ordered symbolism through which he may *know* the common and the ideal reality in a single imaginative act. One would like to linger upon the possible reasons for this. I suspect that evidence from another source, which I shall point out later, will be more telling than anything, even this stanza, that we can find in the odes. The consciousness of change and decay, which can, and did in Keats, inform one of the great modes of poetry, is deeply involved with his special attitude towards sexual love. He never presents love directly and dramatically; it is in terms of Renaissance tapestry, as in "The Eve of St. Agnes," or in a fable of Italian violence, as in "Isabella"; or, most interesting of all, in terms of a little myth, Lamia the snake-woman, a symbol which permits Keats to objectify the mingled attraction and repulsion which his treatment of love contains. I sometimes think that for this reason "Lamia" is his best long poem: the symbol inherently contains the repulsive element, but keeps it at a distance, so that he does not have to face it in terms of common experience, his own, or as he was aware of it in his age. Is it saying too much to suppose that Keats's acceptance of the pictorial method is to a large extent connected with his unwillingness to deal with passion dramat-ically? (There is sensuous detail, but no sensation as direct ex-perience, such as we find in Baudelaire.)

I need not labor a point which even the Victorian critics and biographers, almost without exception, remarked: Keats, both before and during his fatal illness (as other poets have been who were not ill at all) was filled with the compulsive image of the identity of death and the act of love (for example, "You must be mine to die upon the rack if I want you," he wrote to Fanny Brawne); and it is only an exaggeration of emphasis to say that death and love are interchangeable terms throughout his poet-ry. The "ecstasy" that the nightingale pours forth contains the Elizabethan pun on "die" with the wit omitted, and a new semi-mystical intensity of feeling added. And is it too much to say that Keats's constant tendency was to face the moment of love only in terms of an ecstasy so intense that he should not sur-vive it? When Lamia vanishes Lycius "dies." And this affir-mation of life through death is the element that Keats "adds on to things as perceived." But life-in-death is presented pictorially, in space, as an eternal moment, not as a moment of dramatic action in time, proceeding from previous action and looking towards its consequences.

The dialectical tension underlying "Ode to a Nightingale" seems to me to be incapable of resolution, first in terms of Keats's mind as we know it from other sources, and, secondly, in terms of the pictorial technique which dominates the poetic method. This method, which seems to reflect a compulsive necessity of Keats's experience, allows him to present the thesis of his dilem-ma, the ideality of the nightingale symbol, but not the antith-esis, the world of common experience, which is the substance of stanza three. The "resolution" is suspended in the intensity of the images setting forth the love-death identity and reaching a magnificent climax in stanza six ("Now more than ever seems

it rich to die," &c.). But the climax contains a little less than
the full situation; it reaches us a little too simplified, as if Keats
were telling us that the best way to live is to die, or the best way
to die is to live intensely so that we may die intensely. There
may be concealed here one of the oldest syntheses of Christian
thought, that we die only to live; but, if so, there has been a
marked shrinkage in range of that conception since Donne
wrote his "A Nocturnall upon S. Lucies Day."

Messrs. Brooks and Warren, in their excellent if somewhat
confident analysis* of the Nightingale ode, argue with much
conviction that the dramatic frame of the poem, the painful ac-
cession to the trance in the opening lines and the return to immediate reality ("Do I wake or sleep?") at the end, provides a
sufficient form. I confess that I am not sure. I am not certain of
the meaning of what happens inside the frame; but at times I
am not certain that it is necessary to understand it. There is no
perfection in poetry. All criticism must in the end be compara-
tive (this does not mean critical relativity); it must constantly
refer to what poetry has accomplished in order to estimate what
it can accomplish, not what it ought to accomplish; we must
heed Mr. Ransom's warning that perfect unity or integration
in a work of art is a critical delusion. "Ode to a Nightingale"
is by any standard one of the great poems of the world. Our
philosophical difficulties with it are not the same as Keats's
imaginative difficulties, which pertain to the order of experience
and not of reason. The poem is an emblem of one limit of our
experience: the impossibility of synthesising, in the order of experience, the antinomy of the ideal and the real, and, although
that antinomy strikes the human mind with a different force in
different ages (Donne's dualism is not Keats's), it is sufficiently
common to all men in all times to be understood.

If we glance at "Ode on a Grecian Urn," we shall see Keats
trying to unify his pictorial effects by means of direct philosophical statement. "Do I wake or sleep?" at the end of the Nightingale ode asks the question: Which is reality, the symbolic

*Brooks and Warren,
Understanding Po-
etry, pp. 409-415.

nightingale or the common world? The famous Truth-Beauty synthesis at the end of the "Grecian Urn" contains the same question, but this time it is answered. As Mr. Kenneth Burke sees it, Truth is the practical scientific world and Beauty is the ideal world above change. The "frozen" figures on the urn, being both dead and alive, constitute a scene which is at once perceptible and fixed. "This transcendent scene," says Mr. Burke, "is the level at which the earthly laws of contradiction no longer prevail."* The one and the many, the eternal and the passing, the sculpturesque and the dramatic, become synthesised in a higher truth. Much of the little that I know about this poem I have learned from Mr. Burke and Mr. Cleanth Brooks, who have studied it more closely than any other critics; and what I am about to say will sound ungrateful. I suspect that the dialectical solution is Mr. Burke's rather than Keats's, and that Mr. Brooks's "irony" and "dramatic propriety" are likewise largely his own.§ Mr. Brooks rests his case for the Truth-Beauty paradox on an argument for its "dramatic propriety"; but this is just what I am not convinced of. I find myself agreeing with Mr. Middleton Murry (whom Mr. Brooks quotes), who admits that the statement is out of place "in the context of the poem itself." I would point to a particular feature, in the last six lines of stanza four, which I feel that neither Mr. Burke nor Mr. Brooks has taken into a certain important kind of consideration. Here Keats tells us that in the background of this world of eternal youth there is another, from which it came, and that this second world has thus been emptied and is indeed a dead world:

> *What little town by river or sea-shore*
> *Or mountain-built with peaceful citadel,*
>   *Is emptied of this folk, this pious morn?*
> *And, little town, thy streets for evermore*
> *Will silent be; and not a soul to tell*
>   *Why thou art desolate, can e'er return.*

Mr. Burke quite

* *"Symbolic Action in a Poem by Keats,"* Accent, *vol. iv, no. 1, p. 42.*

§ *"History Without Footnotes,"* The Sewanee Review, *vol. lii, no. 1, pp. 89-101.*

rightly sees in this passage the key to the symbolism of the entire poem. It is properly the "constatation" of the tensions of the imagery. What is the meaning of this perpetual youth on the urn? One of its meanings is that it is perpetually anti-youth and anti-life; it is in fact dead, and "can never return." Are we not faced again with the same paradox we had in the Nightingale ode, that the intensest life is achieved in death? Mr. Burke brings out with great skill the erotic equivalents of the life-death symbols; and for his analysis of the developing imagery throughout we owe him a great debt. Yet I feel that Mr. Burke's own dialectical skill leads him to consider the poem, when he is through with it, a phil ·ophical discourse; but it is, if it is anything (and it is a great deal), what is ordinarily known as a work of art. Mr. Burke's elucidation of the Truth-Beauty proposition in the last stanza is the most convincing dialectically that I have seen; but Keats did not write Mr. Burke's elucidation; and I feel that the entire last stanza, except the phrase "Cold Pastoral" (which probably ought to be somewhere else in the poem) is an illicit commentary added by the poet to a "meaning" which was symbolically complete at the end of the preceding stanza, number four. Or perhaps it may be said that Keats did to some extent write Mr. Burke's elucidation; that is why I feel that the final stanza (though magnificently written) is redundant and out of form.

To the degree that I am guilty with Mr. Burke of a prepossession which may blind me to the whole value of this poem (as his seems to limit his perception of possible defects) I am not qualified to criticise it. Here, towards the end of this essay, I glance back at the confession, which I made earlier, of the distance and detachment of my warmest admiration for Keats. It is now time that I tried to state the reasons for this a little more summarily, in a brief comparison of the two fine odes that we have been considering.

Both odes are constructed pictorially in spatial blocks, for the eye to take in serially. Though to my mind this method is better

I

suited to the subject of the Grecian Urn, which is itself a plastic
object, than to the Nightingale ode, I take the latter, in spite of
the blemishes of detail (only some of which we have looked at),
to be the finer poem. If there is not so much in it as in the Grecian
Urn for the elucidation of verbal complexity, there is nowhere
the radical violation of its set limits that one finds in the last
stanza of the Grecian Urn:

> *Thou shalt remain, in midst of other woe*
> *Than ours, a friend to man, to whom thou say'st,*
> *Beauty is truth, truth beauty,—that is all*
> *Ye know on earth, and all ye need to know.*

It is here that the poem gets out of form, that the break in "point
of view" occurs; and if it is a return to Samuel Johnson's dislike of "Lycidas" (I don't think it is) to ask how an urn can say
anything, I shall have to suffer the consequences of that view.
It is Keats himself, of course, who says it; but "Keats" is here
not implicit in the structure of the poem, as he is in "Ode to a
Nightingale"; what he says is what the mathematicians call an
extrapolation, an intrusion of matter from another field of discourse, so that even if it be "true" philosophically it is not a
visible function of what the poem says. With the "dead" mountain citadel in mind, could we not phrase the message of the
urn equally well as follows: Truth is *not* beauty, since even art
itself cannot do more with death than preserve it, and the beauty
frozen on the urn is also dead, since it cannot move. This "pessimism" may be found as easily in the poem as Keats's comforting paradox. So I should return to the Nightingale ode for its
superior *dramatic* credibility, even though the death-life antinomy is not more satisfactorily resolved than in the Grecian Urn.
The fall of the "I" of the poem into the trance-like meditation
in the first stanza and the shocked coming to at the end *ground*
the poem in imaginable action, so that the dialectics of the nightingale symbol do not press for resolution. So I confess a reserved
agreement with Brooks and Warren.

The outlines of the conflicting claims of the ideal and the actual, in Keats's mind, I have touched upon; but now, with the two great odes in mind, I wish to give those hints a somewhat greater range and try, if possible, to point towards the *kind* of experience with which Keats was dealing when he came up short against the limit of his sensibility, the identity of love and death, or the compulsive image of erotic intensity realising itself in "dying."

IV. One of Keats's annotations to Burton's *Anatomy*, in the copy given him by Brown in 1819, in the great period, is as follows:

Here is the old plague spot; the pestilence, the raw scrofula. I mean there is nothing disgraces me in my own eyes so much as being one of a race of eyes nose and mouth beings in a planet call'd the earth who all from Plato to Wesley have always mingled goatish winnyish lustful love with the abstract adoration of the deity. I don't understand Greek—is the love of God and the Love of women express'd by the same word in Greek? I hope my little mind is wrong—if not I could ... Has Plato separated these lovers? Ha! I see how they endeavour to divide—but there appears to be a horrid relationship.* **I am indebted to a note in Colvin, op. cit., p. 549, for the hint which led me to this bitter confession. It appears in Forman, The Complete Works of John Keats, iii, p. 268.*

Keats had just read in Burton the chapter "Love-Melancholy" in which the two Aphrodites, Urania and Pandemos, appear: § *§ Modern readers will find the passage in the edition of Dell and Jordan-Smith (New York, 1927), p. 620.* there is no evidence that he ever knew more about them than this quotation indicates. Professor Thorpe valiantly tries to show us that Keats must have known from his literary environment something of Plato's doctrine of love, but there is no reason to believe that he ever felt the imaginative shock of reading *The Symposium*, and of experiencing first hand an intuition of a level of human experience that the Western world, through Platonism and Christianity, had been trying for more than two millennia to reach. He apparently never knew that the two Aphrodites were merely the subject of Pausanias's speech, one of the preliminaries to Socrates's great dialectical synthesis. The curious thing about Keats's education is that it was almost entirely literary; he had presumably read very little philosophy and religion. He used the Greek myths, not for the complete (if pagan) religious experience in them, but to find a static and sculpturesque emblem of time-less experience—his own and the experience of his age; hence the pictorial method, and hence the necessity for that method.

In my reading of Keats I see his mind constantly reaching to-wards and recoiling from the experience, greatly extended, which is represented by the ambivalent Aphrodite. The conclusion of the sonnet "Bright Star!...":

> *Still, still to hear her tender-taken breath,*
> *And so live ever—or else swoon to death...*

is not Keats's best poetry, but it states very simply the conflict of emotion the symbolic limit of which I have tried to see in terms of the double goddess. The immanence of the Uranian in the Pandemic goddess was not beyond the range of Keats's intellect, but it was at any rate, at the time of his death, imaginatively beyond his reach. His goddess, in so far as she is more than a decorative symbol in Keats, was all Uranian; and to say in an-other way what I have already said, his faulty taste (which is probably at its worst in one of the lines in "Bright Star!...") lies in his inability to come to terms with her Pandemic sister. His pictorial and sculpturesque effects, which arrest time into space, tend to remove from experience the dramatic agitation of Aphrodite Pandemos, whose favors are granted and whose woes are counted in the actuality of time. (There is, of course, a great deal more in Keats than this obsessive symbol through which I see him; and there is also less of the symbol, explicitly presented, than my discussion would indicate; there are only eleven references to "Venus" in all Keats's poetry—he never calls her Aphrodite—and in no instance is very much done with her

symbolically. She has only a fresh Botticellian surface; and one
may observe that she is not mentioned in "Ode to Psyche.")

This "horrid relationship" between the heavenly and earthly
Aphrodites had been in effect the great theme of St. Augustine,
and before him of Lucretius; and it was to inform dramatically
The Divine Comedy. It was perhaps the great achievement of the
seventeenth-century English poets to have explored the relations
of physical and spiritual love; of this Keats seems oblivious;
yet we must admit that an awareness of the imaginative and
spiritual achievements of the past would not have ensured them
to him, as our own excessive awareness fails to ensure them to
us. In Keats's mind there was, as I have said (why it should
have had, even in so young a man, an exclusive dominance I
do not know)—there was, to put it in the simplest language, a
strong compulsion towards the realisation of physical love, but
he could not reconcile it with his idealisation of the beloved.
So we get what has been supposed to be a characteristically romantic attitude—that to *die* at the greatest intensity of love is to
achieve that intensity without diminution. If this is the romantic
attitude—and there is no reason to believe that Wordsworth's
domestic pieties and evasions, or Shelley's rhetorical Godwin-
ism and watered-down Platonism, ever achieved *as experience* a
higher realisation of the central human problem than Keats did
—if this is romanticism, then romanticism (or romantic poetry)
represents a decline in insight and in imaginative and moral
power. In the interval between

> So must pure lovers soules descend
> T'affections, and to faculties,
> Which sense may reach and apprehend,
> Else a great Prince in prison lies . . .

and this:

> But Love has pitched his mansion in
> The place of excrement;
> For nothing can be sole or whole
> That has not been rent . . .

—between Donne and Yeats there was evidently a shrinkage in the range and depth of Western man's experience, as that experience was expressed in works of the imagination, and not merely in the Goethean or Wordsworthian goodwill towards comprehensiveness or the inclusion of a little of everything. Keats seems to me to have been, in England at any rate, the master of the central experience of his age. His profound honesty, his dislike of system and opinion as substitutes for what the imagination is actually able to control, and his perfect artistic courage, will keep him not only among the masters of English poetry but among the few heroes of literature. To apply to Keats a remark of Eliot's about Arnold, I should say that he did not know, because he lacked the maturity to know, the boredom; he knew a little of the horror; but he knew much of the glory, of human life.

—1945

STEPHEN SPENDER'S *POEMS*

MR. Stephen Spender's book contains thirty-three poems that will have a distinct influence upon his contemporaries, not only in England but, I believe, in the United States where for the last twenty years the best verse in the English language has been written. Mr. Spender's originality though limited is genuine; his range as yet is slight, but his quality is not surpassed by any other English poet since the war. For one thing, he has not been compelled to circumvent Eliot in order to speak for himself. Within the general terms of the intellectual crisis of the age, Spender has defined a personal crisis of his own; he begins a solution of the problem in the only way that art is capable of solutions—by giving the problem a fundamental restatement. There is a danger, however, that the meaning of this quality in Spender's work will be missed for a time: his faults will certainly be imitated, his "philosophy" (as such) mistaken for his style, and a kind of rambling accumulation of sensitive perceptions (see poem XXXII) will become the latest mode of Communist verse.

It is one of the defects of revolutionary thought, in this age, so far as poetry is concerned, that it is not assimilable to any great body of sensuous forms. It was possible for Shelley to imagine, at least, that he was rewriting the classical mythology. Our own contemporaries have the gospel according to Father Marx, certain passages of which are almost as moving as Dickens; most of it is merely engaging dialectically, leaving the young humanitarian to flounder in an opaque mass of abstraction that is not easily translated into the mere physical objects that the distressed Platonist, in all times, is compelled to see. The raw initiate into the Society of Friends would suffer, as poet, a similar disability. In the case of Mr. Spender, there is a tendency to work out his philosophy as he goes along, as if he were making a literal translation of the doctrine into metaphors:

The architectural gold-leaved flower
From people ordered like a single mind,
I build.

Or this:

> *... larger than all the charcoaled batteries*
> *And imaged towers against that dying sky,*
> *Religion stands, the church blocking the sun.*

Such translation probably precedes the creative moment, and the best poetry is probably written by men who are not even aware that it has taken place: the actual expression is the total thought. In these passages, Mr. Spender oscillates between two social relatives that have imposed upon him as poetic absolutes. The verse is didactic and as dead as Blackmore or Ambrose Philips. As social and political men we may, if we choose, select all the provisional absolutes we desire; as poets we must be selected by some absolute. We may then criticize it or even reject it, but we cannot get rid of it; like Lord Tennyson's God, it is nearer than hands and feet.

If there is a single good dogma in poetic criticism it is possibly this: that no philosophy is good enough for a poet unless it is so seasoned in his experience that it has become, like the handling of the gravediggers' skulls, a property of easiness. It is not what a poet "believes" (Mr. Richards' theory) but rather what total attitude he takes towards all aspects of his conduct, that constitutes the "content" side of the æsthetic problem. Belief is a statistical and sociological category as applied to the arts: does the poet believe in the trinity? does he believe in votes for women? There may be an equally good theory that modern poets believe entirely too much—that is to say, more than they can, as poets, understand. One might derive from this slender volume more specific beliefs than from the whole of the *Divine Comedy*, in which "belief" in Mr. Richards' sense of the term does not appear.

It is not necessary to give Mr. Spender's philosophy a name: it has been necessary to describe its function in his work, in order to clear the ground. All his best poems convey *single* emotions. And these single emotions are created, in the sense that a table or a chair is created; they are not believed. Poem XIV ("In 1929") is one of the best, possibly the best in the book, and certainly one of the finest English poems of the century. These lines possess an absolute clarity, a complete mastery of words, that has been absent from English verse since Landor (Mr. Spender's metrics deserves separate discussion: he has obviously studied the later Yeats, but without trying to become Yeats):

Now I suppose that the once envious dead
Have learnt a strict philosophy of clay
After these centuries, to haunt us no longer
In the churchyard or at the end of the lane
Or howling at the edge of the city
Beyond the last beanrows, near the new factory.

It is this quality that should influence the contemporary scene.

—1933

K

AN EXEGESIS ON DR. SWIFT

NOW is the reader exceeding curious to learn, from whence this vapour took its rife which had fo long fet the nations at a gaze, what fecret wheel, what hidden fpring could put into motion fo wonderful an engine? It was afterwards difcovered, that the movement of this whole machine had been directed by an abfent female, whofe eyes had raifed a protuberancy, and before emiffion fhe was removed into an enemy's country. What fhould an unhappy prince do in fuch ticklifh circumftances as thefe? he tried in vain the poet's never-failing receipt of corpora quæque. . . . *Having to no purpofe ufed all peaceable endeavours, the collected parts of the* femen, *raifed and inflamed, became aduft, converted to choler, turned, head upon the fpinal duct, and afcended to the brain: the very fame principle, that in-fluences a* bully *to break the windows of a whore, who has jilted him, natu-rally ftirs up a great prince to raife mighty armies, and dream of nothing but fieges, battles, and victories.*

Now the reader is exceeding curious to learn where so singularly a modern passage is to be found in an author whose style betrays the presence of the eighteenth century. Without any ado I may say that it is in Section IX of "A Tale of a Tub," that section being the famous digression from the adven-tures of Peter, Martin, and Jack, which were once so amusing, into a discourse on the "improvement of madness in a common-wealth," a subject which, as we now know, is worth all the mer-its and vices of all the religions put together. The edition of the work that I quote from is dated London, 1766; my quotation is on page 95, vol. I, where the editor, Mr. John Hawkesworth, informs us by footnote that the gentleman whose protuberancy upset the nations "was Harry the Great of France." His identity is, of course, irrelevant, only that it saves me the labor and the reader the tedium of going over in detail the amazing results of the king's *suppressed desire.* Everyone knows, as a horrid example to our free institutions, the extraordinary career of Henri Quatre who, quite lost to the domestic virtues, could do no better than wish his children a common fowl in the pot of a Sunday.

I must hasten to explain at the outset that Dr. Swift evidently believed all great affairs of state, all conquests and religious reforms, systems of philosophy; in short, all the shining glories of human genius at which credulous men used to wonder, are mere symptoms of madness and are caused by the failure of some men to run smoothly in the *"common forms,"* as the Dean pointedly says. For the lower *vapours* ascend to the brain, and in disguise do all manner of mischief on the pretence of doing great deeds of human good.

Dr. Swift's explanation of Harry's trouble seems to us unexceptionable because it has all the sanction of a whole race of philosophers since his time. The Great Harry was a misfit in his society, in spite of being the head of it, so what could he do to compensate for his failure to run smoothly in the common forms but try to make new forms, bluffing his subjects into thinking the new better than the old, and better for them? We have here in Dr. Swift's analysis of the actions of a great prince, a wonderful anticipation of the modern science of psychoanalysis, as this is understood by everybody but the man who invented it, and we are all astonishment that so ignorant a century as the benighted eighteenth, which stood in awe of ancient learning, came up a moment, so to speak, for air, and permitted the fanciful pen of the Dean of St. Patrick's who himself was mad, and ran but poorly in the common forms, to strike out in one of those bold truths that are among us the property and comfort of every reader of the Nashville *Tennessean, This Quarter,* the Chicago *Tribune,* and the New York *Times.*

But to return to the king's protuberancy: though it could have been nothing extraordinary. All are alike, that is scientifically speaking: for all proceed from the same flaw in our nature, to the same ends. Now the only notable features of the king's story are the absenting of the female (who in our more auspicious time is always present) and the failure of that remedy which the Dean modestly calls *corpora quæque*. In fact, the disease with all its public calamities was caused by the king's curious delusion that only this particular one would do. Dr. Swift, as anybody can see, believed the delusion to be ridiculous, and we read between the lines the opinion that the upheaval of France in those times would have been avoided by the exercise of a little modern science—by, in brief, or perhaps not so briefly after all—by the falling back of the king on to the *common form,* which in his case was the common woman, or the woman in common, who is woman-in-general mercifully if paradoxically provided by nature for the relief of the aforesaid natural flaw. It was absurd of the king to feel any preference for the absent woman, and to remain irreconcilable in his choice. The king lacked the Dean's insight into modern science; he failed to see that his malady was not the loss of any particular lady; and he never had sense enough to understand that he had a mere general case of repression, that might have been released, not by forming a secondary preference which is the same delusion in lower degree, but in the wise modern fashion, therapeutically on *corpora quæque.* It is the peculiar glory of our time to have discovered that men do not have particular desires, made up of special qualities of sense that seize the long-slain chimera *imagination,* but only a certain quantity of passions that we may conveniently let off like so much steam.

For in the case of our male concupiscence, it requires only an abstract Female Organ, just as the steam pent up in a boiler requires a pipe, any old pipe so it be of the right size, to let the vapours through. The "collected part" of the steam, not having any orifice to get through owing to the boiler's conceit that this steam was meant to run only one engine in the world, became "raifed and inflamed," and exploded as the history of Harry the Great.

It is proper to remark here the Dean's ingenuity in finding out, however dimly, the great truth of modern life, that everything is common. He did not do, of course, what we have no right to

expect of a simple man, who fooled away his time at theology
and the ancients—he did not show us all the inferences imbed-
ded in the miraculous but incomplete vision that he had, there
being no psychological science at that time with systematic terms
to set all the vision forth. Most of it was choked in his head for
not being aired by the proper words. It is a source of pride to
me as a convinced modern that I know better than Dr. Swift
what he was talking about, and I can look back on the quaint
words used, those vapours and humours, with some astonishment that men living a bare two centuries ago could know so
little, and that genius like the Dean's could be stifled, like that of
Henry James and Mark Twain, by so pervasive an ignorance.

That all things are common is a truth so self-evident that I may
be excused from arguing it: besides I suspect that most readers
know the terms of the argument better than I do. But I beg leave
to defend the truth with some *sidelong shots*
at its detractors, who, though they are rather
uncommon nowadays, have even presumed
out of a wilful aversion from knowledge and
a sense of being *misfits* in a commonwealth
that this truth binds with hoops of steel,—I
say they have had the very gall to pretend that
Dr. Swift did not have prescience of the modern truth when he set forth the causes of King
Henry's greatness; which were nothing but
pruriency.

The sceptics are so fatuous as to believe him to have been
really great, and to believe the Dean thought him so too. They
argue that Dr. Swift was writing a "fatyre" on the general follies
of mankind, without going so far as to impugn the quality of
any individual man; whereas we know that mankind in the
lump has no faults, but rather is the individual weak in not being
able to live up to mankind in general, which is common man.
And the best they can do to support their sophistry is to distort,
as the present writer and other critics of the HUMANISTS have

done, a quotation from Swift himself, who would seem to give the color of authority to their argument; the quotation being that "fatyr, being levelled at all, is never refented for an offenfe by any." They say that the Dean never believed the protuberancy to have caused the trouble, but pretended he did in order iron-ically to assert such a belief to be held by common men, who are the *vulgus*, the herd, the masses old or new, or the natural man. They even say that he hoped to make the common view of great-ness, of which we know the real virtue, ridiculous, by a mock acceptance of it as his own.

There are several grave considerations that render preposter-ous the view held by the sceptical misfits; I offer them not for their novelty, but to put them down for reference. I take the most difficult first, because some metaphysical refinement of defini-tion is required for it, and that is a pest to be rid of in a hurry. Now *even granting* that the sceptics are right in believing the Dean merely tweaked the nose of common opinion, still it is a com-monplace of history that truth comes unbeckoned and often, as it were, by accident: *the Dean of St. Patrick's thought better than he knew.* The Dean's intention was the mere irrelevant mode of truth, not the substance—a profound distinction. Moreover—and this completely routs the sceptic on this point—the history of society since 1700 (or 1697?) has vindicated, validated, and, of late, syndicated as seriously true what Dr. Swift possibly wrote of Henri Quatre in bitter jest. And this, as the wise William James, wiser than his brother Henry, said, makes truth true.

The second argument to refute the misfits will, of course, meet opposition only from the men of that kidney themselves: it leaves them out as a minority—those dissidents justly contemptible to the modern mind. It is, that the consensus of men has taken in the last few generations a species of popular vote on Truth, and discovered it to be what the majority believe; or rather, for con-venience, it was decided beforehand that what the majority believed would be truth. We can only pause here briefly, to wonder at the stupidity of past ages in not devising this simple, infallible and irrefutable method of ascertaining what is true; so much better and more conclusive than the devious way of *think-ing out* the truth, practised in the past; and having as the final sanction the maxim that figures, mainly a majority of figures, cannot lie.

We have arrived at the third and overwhelming refutation. What we know to be true—that everything is common—has always been held by most men, and it is owing to the wicked tyr-anny of rulers and priests, along with their legion of Belial who call themselves gentlemen and philosophers, that this truth in the past was robbed of its impressive vindication by vote, and kept in a mean and clownish condition. We have learned what a social parasite and cancer the class of philosophers were, for we hear automobile salesmen, bond dealers (I believe they are called), steel manufacturers, bankers, communists, managers of rubber factories, stock brokers, and the indispensable workers who thrive on shaking hands with these, pronounce not only on the meaning of Aristotle better than Avicenna or Aquinas, but rightly go on to dispense with him utterly, giving the new truth in common terms, as they see it; for they are prepared to exhibit the truths that *work out*. They have forever exposed the sham distinction of the sceptics, who look to the *past,* as the com-pensatory snobbery of misfits. They have forever exposed the evil dogma of the philosophers that traders such as they are, dealing in money only (the archetype of the figures that do not lie), or passing through their own hands the produce garnered by oth-ers, are cancers and parasites. It is evident that the philosophers historically called the traders blood-suckers, in order to give the odor of virtue to their own thirst for power.

And here I cannot commend too highly the modern temper-ance in social affairs. Instead of violently and after the manner of ancient-statesmen putting the heirs of the philosophers to death, or breaking them as a class, as Henry VIII did the monks, the Business Body, or *corpus negotii,* as government is now called, permits them to go on talking and writing, since no one pays

them any mind. They are laughed at as parasites, but with kind-
ness because they are harmless; and if they eat and occupy space,
the drain on the public is small, because they eat little like the
poor whites in the South, who were said to eat Hagerstown
clay, and usually bring up a large family in two rooms. And
thus they hang themselves, as it were, by getting more trivial every day, and counting for less, not being worth killing; so that
they are as innocent as the vast museum collections in great cities,
that people stare at occasionally whether at a saurian's tooth or
the Magna Carta, as at some momento of ancient folly.

The reader will complain—it is my farthest wish to offend the
reader—that I have not made clear beyond doubt what I mean
by saying that Dr. Swift foretold our belief that all is common:
I have shown, I hope, that this truth came of a popular vote,
but I have not yet said fully what it is. Nor shall I tell. If the
reader complain, I will rejoin that the modern truth is better
known than acknowledged, and too much definition is a sign
of madness.

For a second glance at the Dean's remarks on Harry will yield
up the gist of the matter. It is that "the very same principle that
influences a *bully* to break the windows of a
whore, who has jilted him, naturally stirs up
a great prince to raise mighty armies." Not to
clutter an exegesis with too much quotation,
I may say for the Dean that it also stirs up a
philosopher to invent a system, or a poet to
write an epic: the Dean expressly mentions a
little further on Monsieur Des Cartes—who-
ever he was—but if it were a protuberancy, in
his case, or a jilt, or both, it is not explained.
Now the identity of the bully with the prince,
the philosopher and the poet, is the great modern truth, which
has been held by the bully, repressed, unarticulated, and made
clownish, for many ages up to now.

There is a single flaw in the general acceptance that the truth has received, but it is, I hasten to add, due strictly to a flaw in our nature, now rapidly being overcome, rather than to any fault of this high truth itself. As was to be expected in a period of transition from a dark age to an age of enlightenment, people still held on to some of the outward shows that went with the delusion of the uncommon. For example, when the bully understood that his truth prevailed, authorizing him to lead society, he foolishly tried to join his truth up with the superficial cast of a gentleman, or the mode of an exploded pseudo-truth. This was the painful experience of men in the recent past, like Mr. Carnegie or Mr. Frick, or the interesting person who stole the Erie railroad, and cried: "Nothing is lost, save honor," meaning that he had the hat, stick, gloves and carriage, and the large collection of paintings, of a gentleman without the outmoded honor.

It was only this mistake of retaining superficies, as if Blackbeard had walked his quarter-deck in a bishop's mitre, that gave the transition man a hue of knavery; he did one thing supposing he was doing another. There are hopeful signs, however, of which the career of Mr. Capone is the brightest, that the bully (quaint word!) has found the mode proper to his essence, unlike Mr. Frick and Dr. Swift, and will no longer try to pretend that he is something else, that is discredited by all men. In the future his conduct will be unalloyed, and virtuous—which is to say, common. The problem that vexed the Dean—what to do with madness, or uncommonness, in a *common*wealth is solved. For we know that "Paradise Lost" is a failure in the common form, the author perhaps never finding the right wife, being blind, as if in that condition any woman wouldn't do.

—1931

L

LONGINUS

TO BEGIN an essay with a silent apology to the subject is commendable, but one should not expect the reader to be inter-ested in it. I allude to the ignorance in which I had underesti-mated Longinus, before I reread him after twenty years, because I am convinced that it is typical. Who reads Longinus? I do not mean to say literally that he is not read. There is an excellent recent study by Mr. Elder Olson; there are the fine books by Mr. T. R. Henn and Mr. Samuel H. Monk,* which persons of the critical interest should know something about and doubtless do. Until these books appeared, there had been no serious con-sideration of Longinus since Saintsbury's *A History of Criticism* (1900). In some twenty-five years of looking at criticism in the United States and England, I have not seen, with the exceptions already noticed, a reference to the περὶ ὕψους which is of more than historical interest. One might, with misplaced antiquarian zeal, find the name, if not much more, of Aristotle in the pages of a fashionable journal like *Horizon*; one would have to go to the learned journals, which few critics see, to find even the name of Longinus. Until Mr. Henn and Mr. Monk reminded us of him, he had been dropped out of active criticism since the end of the eighteenth century. I should like to believe that these ex-cellent scholars have brought about a Longinian revival. Mr. Herbert Read informs me that Coleridge in *Table Talk* spoke of him as "no very profound critic." It must seem to us today that Coleridge buried him in that remark. I am not confident that I shall succeed where Mr. Monk and Mr. Henn failed (if they did fail), that what I am about to say will exhume Longinus.

* Longinus and English Criticism, by T. R. Henn (Cam-bridge, 1934); and The Sublime: A Study of Critical Theories in XVIII-Century England, by Samuel H. Monk (New York, 1935).

I.   This is not the occasion to establish a correct English title for περὶ ὕψους. (In the New Testament ὕψος means not the physical heavens [οὐρανος] but something like "on high.") To my mind, the idea of height or elevation contained in the title, *Of the Height of Eloquence,* which was given to the work by the first English translator, John Hall, in 1652, is more exact than *On the Sublime,* which carries with it the accretions of Boileau and the English eighteenth century, and the different meanings contributed later by Burke and Kant, which are far removed from anything that I have been able to find in this third (or is it first?) century treatise. So far from Kant's is Longinus's conception of "sublimity" that one pauses at the marvelous semantic history of the term. In Chapter IX Longinus quotes a passage from the *Iliad,* Book XX, about the war of the gods, and comments: "Yet these things terrible as they are, if they are not taken as an allegory are altogether blasphemous and destructive of what is seemly." To allegorize infinite magnitude, quantity beyond the range of the eye, is to reduce it to the scale of what Kant called the Beautiful as distinguished from the Sublime. The "sublimity" of the passage, in the Kantian sense, Longinus could not accept. These shifts of meaning are beyond the scope of my interest and my competence. Three other brief and confusing parallels will fix in our minds the difficulties of Longinus's title. His insight, perhaps unique in antiquity, which is contained in the distinction between the "persuasion" of oratory and the "transport" of what, for want of a better phrase, one may call the literary effect, reappears in this century as neo-symbolism and surrealism. Some twenty years ago the Abbé Bremond decided that "transport" meant religious mysticism, and wrote a book called *La Poésie pure.* In England, about thirty years ago, Arthur Machen, of whom few people of the generations younger than mine have heard, the author of *The Hill of Dreams* and other novels after Huysmans, wrote a small critical book called *Hieroglyphics.* Machen proposed to discern the real thing in literature with a test that he called "ecstasy," but what made Machen ecstatic left many persons cold. At any rate, the Greek word in Longinus that we translate as "transport" is ἔκστασις. Had Boileau not stuffed Longinus with neo-classical "authority," would he have been discovered by the French and English romantics, to whom he could have spoken from another if equally wrong direction?

This topic may be dropped with the observation that literary history is no more orderly than any other history.

I shall, then, in the following remarks, think of the two key terms in Longinus, ὕψος and ἔκστασις, as respectively Elevation of Language and Transport; but I cannot expect to disentangle them from each other. They contain, in their interrelations, a version of a persistent ambiguity of critical reference which appeared with Aristotle, had vigorous life up to Coleridge (with whom it comes back disguised), and now eggs on the edifying controversy of the contemporary English and American critics: Ransom, Cleanth Brooks, Read, Leavis, Richards, Blackmur, and Winters. Is Elevation an objective quality of the literary work? Is Transport its subjective reference denoting the emotions of the reader—or the "hearer," as Longinus calls him—as he receives the impact of Elevation? Does either term, Elevation or Transport, point to anything sufficiently objective to be isolated for critical discussion?

This is not the moment to answer that question, if I were competent to answer it. Our first duty is to find out how Longinus asks it. After defining Elevation tautologically, in Chapter I, as "a kind of supreme excellence of discourse" (ἐξοχή τις λόγων ἐστὶ τὰ ὕψη), he describes its effect:

For what is out of the common *affects the hearer not to persuade but to entrance* (οὐ γὰρ εἰς πειθὼ τοὺς ἀκροωμένους ἀλλ᾽ εἰς ἔκστασιν ἄγει τὰ ὑπερφυᾶ). *It moves to wonder and surprise, and always wins against what is merely delightful or persuasive. It is not enough in one or two passages of a work to exhibit invention schooled by experience, nor again the fine order and distribution of its parts, nor even these qualities displayed throughout. Rather, I suggest, does the sublime, fitly expressed, pierce everything like a flash of lightning. . . .*

* With the exception of a few phrases I quote throughout from the translation by Frank Granger (London, 1935), which seems to me the most perspicuous English version. The exceptions are the result of a collation of the Granger and other versions with what is probably the definitive scholarly translation, by W. Rhys Roberts (Cambridge, 1899). All the modern translations render ὕψος as "sublime," and it has obviously been necessary to keep the word when it occurs in a quoted passage.

Not to persuade, but to entrance, like a flash of lightning. In these words Longinus breaks with the rhetoricians who had dominated ancient criticism since Aristotle, four to six hundred years before him, and who continued to dominate it until the seventeenth century. Neither Longinus nor Dante, on *De Vulgari Eloquentia,* had any influence on critical theory after them, until the time of Boileau, when Longinus was used to justify rules that he had never made; Dante's criticism has languished in the department of biography; at best, in the history of criticism, as a document of the time.

II. Chapter II opens with the question: "We must first discuss whether there is an art of the sublime." In the Greek, the phrase is ὕψους τις ἢ βάθους τέχνη—"an art of height or of depth"; but the word we should attend is τέχνη, "art," which the Greeks used for any teachable skill, from metal-working to music and medicine. They applied the term to all the skills of making for which an objective rationale could be devised. Longinus explains the views of Cæcilius, the opponent of uncertain identity whom the περὶ ὕψους was written to refute, who believed that elevation of language came through nature alone, that the great writer, born great, needs nothing but his birth. In this controversy of lively acrimony with a man who may have been dead three hundred years (such was the leisure of antiquity), Longinus at the beginning of his essay opposes, in opposing Cæcilius, both the Platonic and the Aristotelian doctrines, and holds that style is a compound of natural talent and conscious method. He thus parts with Plato's "divine madness" in the *Ion,* and implicitly claims for Thought and Diction, two of the nonstructural elements in Aristotle's analysis of tragedy, a degree of objectivity that Aristotle's rhetorical view of poetic language could not include.

If literary method cannot alone produce a style, the judgment of which, says Longinus, "is the last fruit of long experience," it can "help us to speak at the right length and to the occasion." How much interpretation of a casual observation such as this, which is only common sense, the modern scholiast is entitled to develop, I do not know. Although Longinus may have in mind merely the orator and the *public* occasion, may we just see him reaching out for a criterion of objectivity for any sort of literary composition? The "right length" is the adaptation of form to subject; and is not the "occasion" the relation between the poet and the person to whom the poem is addressed? We have, foreshadowed here, I think, a principle of dramatic propriety, a sense of the "point of view" in composition, the prime literary strategy which can never be made prescriptive, but which exhibits its necessity equally in its operation and in its lapse. Later, discussing meter, Longinus tells us that Elevation cannot be achieved in the trochaic, or tripping, meter, and we may dismiss the remark as the perennial fallacy which identifies certain fixed effects with certain meters. But if we can imagine "Lycidas" written in trochees and "The Raven" in iambuses, we might suppose the one would be worse, the other considerably better. And if we look at "length" and "occasion" in somewhat different terms, we shall find ourselves again in the thick of one of our own controversies. Does not the occasion force upon the poet the objective and communicable features of his work? Are they not Mr. Winters's theory of the relation of "feeling" to "rational content" and Mr. Ransom's theory of a "texture" within a "structure"?

In exceeding the literal text of Longinus in this matter, I hope that I have not also stretched two living critics into an agreement which they have scarcely acknowledged; nor should I ask them to acknowledge Longinus as their forerunner. I suggest that Longinus's question "Is there an art of Elevation?" is the question we are asking today, somewhat as follows: can there be a criticism of convincing objectivity which approaches the literary work through the analysis of style and which arrives at its larger aspects through that aperture?

That is the question of our time. In asking it, are we not fol-lowing Longinus rather than Aristotle? Aristotle began with the conspicuous "larger aspects" of a mature literary genre, Greek tragedy, and got around to the problems of poetic language only at the end, and as a rhetorician (except for one curious remark about metaphor) who offers us shrewd but merely schematic advice about the use of figures.

III.   If there is an art of Elevation, if there is possible a coherent criticism of literature through its language, it follows that we must examine good and bad writers together, in order to arrive, not at rules, but at that "judgment of style which is the fruit of long experience"; to arrive at that sense of the length and the occasion which will permit us, as poets, to imitate not Homer's style but its excellence, in our own language. It is here that in-tensive literary criticism and literary tradition work together; it is here that we arrive at the idea of a literary tradition which does not enjoin the slavery of repetition, but the emulation which comes of insight. We shall have of course to deal as best we can with the ambiguity of Longinus's word τέχνη. By the "art of height or of depth" does he mean criticism? Or does he mean the "art" of the poet? He means, I take it, both; and it is proper that he should. For our sense of the achievement of the past may issue in a critical acquisition of knowledge which is not to be put away in the attic when the creative moment comes. At this point one may profitably notice two characteristic defects, defects of its quality, that proud and self-sufficient writers fall into in attempting the elevated style. "Frigidity," says Longinus, is the overelaboration of the academic writer, a violation of length due to aiming at "the curious and the artificial." The "feeling" (or the detail) is unreal in the sense that it is on a scale smaller than its intelligible form. Likewise, the opposite fault—and in de-scribing it Longinus has written as good criticism as any that I know, of Thomas Wolfe and the contemporary lyrical novel; he says:

Theodorus calls it the mock-inspired. It is emotion out of place and empty where there is no need of it, or lack of proportion where proportion is needed. Some writers fall into a maudlin mood and digress from their subject into their own tedious emotion. Thus they show bad form and leave their audience unimpressed: necessarily, for they are in a state of rapture, and the audience is not.

If this is the performance of the writer great by nature and beyond "art," Henry James gives us his dreary portrait: "The writer who cultivates his instinct rather than his awareness sits by finally in a stale and shrinking puddle." His awareness of what? I should say of the "occasion" and the "length," the sense of limiting structure and of what, within that limit, is to be objectively communicated and made known. This sense becomes operative through "art," τέχνη, technique, the controlled awareness *through* language of what can be made actual *in* language, resulting in a just, if unpredictable, proportion between what Longinus calls the "emotion" and the "subject." Doubtless, any experienced reader of literature can point to the failures of great writers in the two extremes of disproportion corresponding to two forms of pride that prevent the complete discovery of the subject: the pride of intellect and the pride of feeling, the pride of will and the pride of instinct. (Perhaps the history of the imagination is the pendulum between these extremes.) Mr. Blackmur has shown us in the past few years how the thesis in Dostoevsky distorts or even wrecks the theme, the imaginative actuality in which the form ought to have been discovered under pressure of its internal necessity. In a more recent writer, D. H. Lawrence, we get both extremes of pride: the attack on the intellect in behalf of instinct, instinct itself hardening into a core of abstraction which operates as intellectual pride, as thesis, not as realized form.

The instances of "disproportion" could be multiplied, but I pause to remark my own digression, and to ask, as the eighteenth-century critics seem not to have done, whether there is not already, in what I have said, a certain excess of gloss, commentary cut loose from the text commented upon, a self-indulgence which seems to attribute to the subject a comprehension which one is covertly claiming for oneself? Criticism should no doubt observe the same proprieties of occasion and length that we require of the imagination; but it has seldom done so, and I think with good reason. If criticism is only secondary to literature, it is thus the dependent partner, and for the hazards that it must face in every generation it must constantly worry the past for support, and make too much of what it revives, or perhaps even make it into something different. Perhaps I have got out of the περὶ ὕψους at this stage of the discussion only a general insight available, if not always used, as common property since Coleridge. Yet we should remember that Longinus alone seems to have achieved it in the ancient world.

I have been trying to see the outlines, before I move on to some of the particular judgments in the περὶ ὕψους, of a possible framework into which to put Longinus's profound but topical dialectic. In the same chapter (II) in which the proportions of length and occasion are held to be established through "art" or method, he writes this crucial passage:

Demosthenes says somewhere that in ordinary life luck is the greatest good, and that it cannot exist without another which is not inferior to it, namely prudent conduct. Following him, we might say, in the case of style, that nature takes the place of good luck; and art, of prudent conduct. Most important of all, we must learn from art the fact that some elements of style depend upon nature alone.

At this point four pages of the manuscript disappear, a loss of the first importance to critical theory. If the amateur

M

Hellenist reads from classical criticism a passage in which the word "nature" occurs, he is likely to read it with Boileau or the English eighteenth century, and get entangled in the thickets of "nature" which they opposed to "art," when they were not effecting a compromise by making art nature to advantage dressed; and so on. It seems to me that we ought to support the passage just quoted with a full sense of the special kind of judgment that Longinus brings to bear upon the actual texture of Greek literature; he produces many examples which cannot be cited here. We could then just see in it the first declaration of independence from the practical, forensic eloquence of the rhetoricians.

"Most important of all, we must learn from art the fact that some elements of style depend upon nature alone." In trying to understand this nice oxymoron, I shall take risks which are perhaps not greater than those taken by most commentators on the *Poetics*. Most important of all, I make Longinus say, we learn from the development of technique that stylistic autonomy is a delusion, because style comes into existence only as it discovers the subject; and conversely the subject exists only after it is formed by the style. No literary work is perfect, no subject perfectly formed. Style reveals that which is not style in the process of forming it. Style does not create the subject, it discovers it. The fusion of art and nature, of technique and subject, can never exceed the approximate; the margin of imperfection, of the unformed, is always there—nature intractable to art, art unequal to nature. The converse of Longinus's aphorism will further elucidate it: we must learn from nature that some elements of subject matter, in a literary work, "depend" upon art alone. There is a reciprocal relation, not an identity—not, certainly, the identity of form and content—a dynamic, shifting relation between technique and subject; and they reveal each other. This is my sense of Longinus's primary insight. It is an insight of considerable subtlety that has a special claim to the attention of our generation.

IV. I suppose we should agree that by and large the critical method of the *Poetics* is inductive. Aristotle's generalizations proceed from a scrutiny of one kind of literature, drama, chiefly from one kind of drama, tragedy, and from one kind of tragedy, Greek. Longinus repeats Aristotle's animadversions on "character," which Aristotle seems to think need not be much developed if the "plot" is good. We must constantly remind ourselves of the narrow range of literature at the command of the two great critics of antiquity; they lacked the novel, for one thing, and Aristotle evidently did not consider the works of his great predecessor and teacher worthy of the name of "poetry." The larger conception of a literature does not appear in the *Poetics*. Although Longinus, trained as he must have been in the rhetorical schools, did not see clearly whither he was heading, it is just the awareness of *literature at large* which raises his theory of the relation of language and subject to a higher degree of useful generality than any literary theory before him had reached. He is the first, though necessarily incomplete, literary critic. His question, put again, in its wider implications, is: what distinguishes literature from practical oratory, from history? A quality, he says in effect, beyond an immediate purpose. His discussion of imagination is what we should expect: it is the classical rhetorician's view of the image as a "mental picture," which he, along with his age, seems to believe must be laid on the work discretely from the top. Yet the distinction between two widely different purposes in the controlled use of language puts his doctrine on a high yet accessible level of empirical generalization, and makes it possible for him to look beyond specific conventions to estimate the value of a literature offering a great variety of forms and structures.

It has been supposed by many critics that Longinus is not interested in structure, that his doctrine of "transport" and the "lightning flash" anticipates the romantic *frisson*, or that Pope did it justice when he called in Longinus to help him "snatch a grace beyond the reach of art." I think I have shown that Longinus would reject that art which is beyond its own reach. And

what, in fact, I now wish to show is that Longinus is quite prepared to put his finger directly upon the problem of structure,
and by implication to tell us that structure is not in the formal
"type" or genre, a viable body of special conventions, such as the
lyric, the ode, or the epic provides, but exists in the language
of the poem.

After discussing, in Chapters VIII and IX, the five sources
of Elevation in language (to which I shall return) he analyzes
the effect, in terms of structure, of Sappho's Ode to Anactoria,
beginning: φαίνεταί μοι κῆνος ἴσος θεοῖσιν. The analysis is brief
(everything in Longinus is brief but the lacunæ in the text), yet
it is probably the first example in criticism of structural analysis
of a lyric poem. (I ought for my purpose here to know more than
I do, which is virtually nothing, about the ancient theory of the
Passions.) I quote the entire passage:

*Let us now go on to see whether
we have anything further by means of which we can raise our words to the
sublime. Since, then, in the substance of everything, we find certain elements which naturally belong to it, we should of course find one cause of the
sublime by always choosing the most relevant circumstances and by compounding them (ἐπισυνθέσει) to make, so to speak, one body (ἕν τι σῶμα
ποιεῖν). For the audience is attracted, first by our choice of topics (ὁ μὲν
γὰρ τῇ ἐκλογῇ . . . τῶν λημμάτων), and second, by the conciseness of our
exposition. For example, Sappho takes from their actual setting the feelings that accompany the frenzy of love. Where then
does she display her skill? In the tact with which she
chooses and binds together supreme and intense feelings.*

Peer of Gods he seemeth to me, the blissful
Man who sits and gazes at thee before him,
Close beside thee sits, and in silence hears thee
      Silverly speaking,

Laughing love's low laughter. Oh this, this only
Stirs the troubled heart in my breast to tremble!

For should I but see thee a little moment,
  Straight is my voice hushed;

Yea, my tongue is broken, and through and through me
'Neath the flesh impalpable fire runs tingling;
Nothing see mine eyes, and a noise of roaring
  Waves in my ear sounds;

Sweat runs down in rivers, a tremor siezes
All my limbs, and paler than grass in autumn,
Caught by pains of menacing death, I falter,
  Lost in the love trance. . . .

Do you not wonder how she gives chase at once to soul and body, to words and tongue, to sight and color, all as if scattered abroad, how uniting contradictions,* *she is frozen and burns, she raves and is wise? For either she is panic-stricken or at point of death; she is haunted not by a single emotion but their* whole company.§

I have inserted here W. Rhys Roberts's translation of καθ' ὑπεναντιώσεις because it conveys more accurately the force of the Greek, which means opposite feelings rather than "at variance within," as Granger has it.

§ *Roberts has it "a concourse of passions," which is more accurate. The Greek ἵνα μὴ ἕν τι περὶ αὐτὴν πάθος φαίνηται, παθῶν δὲ σύνοδος is literally a "coming together of roads," a crossroads; so better perhaps than either "their whole company" or a "concourse of passions" are the renditions "a clash of feelings," "a crossing of feelings."*

Towards the end of the περὶ ὕψους there is some scattered commentary on the rhetorical figures; but in the criticism of Sappho
the language is not that of the tropes and figures. In so far as it
concerns emotion, it is "psychological," if not very exact, even
in the terms of the classical psychology of the passions; yet perhaps it is not too much to claim for Longinus's perception of
opposites in this poem, of the positive compulsion given tension
by its negative, that it goes deeper and is more attentive to what
the poem says than anything that Arnold has to say about
Keats's or Milton's poetry. *He is trying to see what is happening in the
poem.* If he is hampered by his affective terms, so was Mr. T. S.
Eliot when, in an early essay, he was getting at a similar play
of opposites (what Mr. Cleanth Brooks has since called "para-

dox") by proposing his theory of the positive and the negative emotion, and more especially the theory of the central "emotion" gathering up and controlling a variety of contingent "feelings." Mr. Eliot's early theory I should call advanced romantic criti⁄ cism: it was struggling through the subjective effect towards the objective structure of the work. Longinus's criticism of Sappho is advanced romantic criticism, as advanced as Mr. Eliot's.

One hesitates to present to Longinus a theory which I hope is not implicit in his phrase ἕν τι σῶμα ποιεῖν, "to make into one body"; it looks like an organic theory of poetry, but if we sup⁄ pose that he is merely using the phrase analogically, and means by it no more than he says a moment later about the poem being a result of choosing and binding together intense feelings, we shall have to acknowledge the presence of a quite modern piece of criticism. At the least, he is telling us that in this poem con⁄ tradictions are united, bound together, not that Sappho was expressing herself. We are a long step on the way to that critical moment when the affective vocabulary goes over into linguistic analysis, when, instead of what the poem feels like, we try to decide what it says. That Longinus was farther along this road than we may at a glance suspect there is evidence in the remark⁄ able sentence that he plumps down before us without explana⁄ tion: "... the sublime is often found where there is no emotion." There will be something to say about this when we come to the discussion of "harmony," or composition.

V. The promise at the beginning of the treatise to produce the elements of an Art of Elevation leads to a good deal of miscella⁄ neous specification, under five heads, for its achievement; but the dialectical links among the categories are not distinct. If we think of Longinus as Pascal's man of *finesse*, man of insights, and of Aristotle as a man of *géométrie*, man of deduction, we shall have to look twice at Mr. Olson's observation that, "Unlike Edmund Burke, who finds the sources of sublimity in qualities of the subject matter of art, Longinus finds them in the faculties

of the author." This is partly true; but it is misleading, if we are
led to suppose that Longinus tried but failed to erect a systematic
philosophy of art, comparable to Burke's *A Philosophical Enquiry
into the Origins of Our Ideas of the Sublime and Beautiful*, but placing
the origins of the ideas in the author. He is ambiguous at this
point, but I have shown, I hope, that his considerable originality
consists in shifting the centre of critical interest, without reject⁄
ing it as an "interest," from the genetic and moral judgment to
the æsthetic, from the subject matter and the psychology of the
author to the language of the work. When he describes the first
of his five sources of Elevation as the "impulse towards what is
great in thought," he speaks perhaps as a casual Platonist, but
primarily as a rhetorician in the great tradition reaching from
Aristotle to Cicero.

In distinguishing a critical insight from the intellectual disci⁄
pline from which, to an extent, it may be a departure, we tend
to assume that the insight has replaced the discipline; whereas it
may merely alter it. It is not certain that we need a philosophical
æsthetics in order to produce a work of art; at the Renaissance,
I need hardly to observe, the education in rhetoric and oratory
produced poets. Sidney is not too apologetic for "straying from
Poertie to Oratorie"; for, he says, "both have such an affinity
in this wordish consideration...." It was the point of view of
his age. Disciplining that point of view was the art of rhetoric,
one member of a tripartite whole completed by ethics and poli⁄
tics; rhetoric was the ethics of the public man in its appropriate
discipline, the art of the enthymeme, or rhetorical syllogism.

The second of Longinus's categories, "strong and inspired
emotion," proceeds from the first, or from a common source; it
also is "due to nature." Here we come upon a curious and, as
usual, undeveloped observation. Strong and inspired emotion
is one source of, but it is not the same as, style. Pity, grief, and
fear, he says, are "humble (ταπεινά: lowly, mean) and without
the note of the Sublime"—as if in "pity" and "fear" he had a
critical eye to Aristotle, whose doctrine of *katharsis* was practical

and even "sociological." The curious observation honors the critic who puts "awareness" above system, for it enters an excep-tion to the rule: "The masters of panegyric," Longinus says, "are seldom given to emotion." What, then, are they given to? An English instance will be helpful. The epigraph to "Lycidas" tells us that "The Author bewails a Learned Friend"—but the author does nothing of the sort;* the strong feeling is directed at the clergy, and even it is sufficiently assimilated into the rich pastoral texture.

I pass over sources two and three, the "framing of rhetorical figures" and "nobility of expression," with the remark that Lon-ginus is prudential, like a good teacher, and on these topics not more rewarding than the rhetoricians, Demetrius and Dionysi-us. But number five, "Composition and distribution of words and phrases into a dignified and exalted unit," heads up the entire argument. "It is a unity of composition," he says, "attained through language." If it is so attained, it is not attained, though it may originate, in the inaccessible nobility of the author's mind. Observe again the superiority of Longinus's insight, with the specific work in mind, to his critical apparatus, which tends to the moralistic and academic. We may see composition here as *ordonnance*, "the best words in the best order." It is more than that. Composition is the total work, not the superaddition of method. Its effect is not to persuade but to entrance; it is "out of the com-mon," not uncommon words, but words used uncommonly well. It is clear that Longinus, by and large, is not recommend-ing the "grand style"; his translators have probably done him a disservice in rendering his characteristic adjective μέγα as "grand"; it is, rather, great, unusual, *uncommon*; and likewise ὕψος, "height," which I understand as "excellence." ἔκστασις is our subjective acknowledgment of the presence of the uncommon, of an objective order of unpredictable distinction. He is quite ex-plicit in this matter. By means of "an appropriate structure, and by this means only, as we have sufficiently shown, the best writ-ers give the effect of stateliness and distinction which is removed

* Mr. John Crowe Ransom made this ob-servation in "A Poem Nearly Anonymous," The World's Body, (Scribner's, 1938), pp. 1-28.

from the commonplace." In illustration he quotes a line from the
Hercules Furens of Euripides:

γέμω κακῶν δὴ κοὐκέτ' ἔσθ' ὅποι τεθῇ
I am loaded with sorrows nor can I take on more.

"The phrase is quite commonplace but it has *gained elevation* by
the arrangement of the words." The fine statement that follows
ought to remove any remaining misconception of the nature of
"transport," if we still suppose it to be the romantic shudder; it
addresses itself to the whole mind:

> ... *if a work of literature fails to
disclose to the reader's intelligence an outlook beyond the range of what is
said, when it dwindles under a careful and continuous inspection, it cannot
be truly sublime, for it has reached the ear alone.... For that is truly grand
(μέγα) of which the contemplation bears repeating.*

There must be, in
short, a total quality of the work which abides its first impact;
to that total quality he gives the name of composition.

It includes rhythm. Saintsbury, whose exposition of Longinus might have revived his influence had somebody else written
it, misses the originality of Longinus's treatment of this subject.
Longinus's location of rhythm in the total composition, as binding and bound up with it, is perhaps the best critical insight of
its kind before Coleridge. Quoting a passage from Demosthenes, he makes the experiment of adding a syllable, and observes
that the "sublime phrase is loosened and undone by lengthening
of the final rhythm." Likewise, if the phrase were shortened by
a syllable. His principle of prose rhythm is negatively stated,
but it seems to me to hold for every kind of writing. It is: prose
rhythm should not have "a conspicuous movement of sound."
It must seem, even if metaphysically it is not, at one with the
meaning; it must not call attention to itself, unless—as in Tacitus,
Gibbon, Doughty, or Sir Thomas Browne—the "conspicuous
movement of sound" is a tonal vehicle that once established is
not distinguishable from, but is part of, the subject itself. But if

N

it is a rhythm "like that of a dancer taking his step before the audience," which the audience anticipates, it distracts attention from what is being said to who is saying it. It is a disproportion in composition similar to that of the orator or the poet who "digresses from the subject into his own tedious emotions." Had Longinus been discussing the rhythm of verse, I should have been able to cite Swinburne and *The Age of Anxiety* by Mr. W. H. Auden.

VI.   I have postponed consideration of the third source of Elevation to this concluding section because it pertains in part to metaphor, the *pons asinorum* of literary criticism. If on this subject Longinus is unsatisfactory, it is only a matter of degree; here everybody is unsatisfactory, even Mr. I. A. Richards, whose *Philosophy of Rhetoric* offers a good deal but promises too much. This is a field of inquiry of a difficulty coördinate with that of the burden of the mystery. Here again Longinus is prudential, but he no doubt gives us as good account as any of the classical precept of nothing-too-much. Don't use too many metaphors, unless you are overwhelmed by emotions which make them credible. Follow Aristotle, perhaps in the *Rhetoric*; soften the metaphor up by inserting "as if" or "just as though" and making it a simile that does not assert improbable identities.

One goes through the περὶ ὕψους, and then the *Rhetoric*, halfheartedly and vainly, looking for something better than this, from the literary point of view, that Longinus might have overlooked, or for something as far-reaching as Aristotle's own Delphic pronouncement in Chapter XXII of the *Poetics*, where he says:

> It is a great thing indeed to make a proper use of these poetical forms, as also of compounds and strange words. But the greatest thing by far is to be a master of metaphor. It is the one thing that cannot be learnt from others; and it is also a sign of genius, since a good metaphor implies an intuitive perception of the similarity in dissimilars.

That is very nearly the

beginning and the end of our own inquiries into metaphor; but I am rash enough to question whether Aristotle, as a Greek, could know, as we have known since Shakespeare and Donne, how similar dissimilars can be made to seem, or (to take an extreme view which is not unknown today) how similar they can be made to *be*. Metaphor, says Aristotle, is the transference of names, through the permutations of genus and species, or by analogy. Metaphor by analogy takes the formula of arithmetical proportion, a quantitative and relational procedure. We are thus in the Greek Cosmos, an ordering of solid objects under a physics of motion, in which the formal object offers but a narrow margin of analogy to any other. If the ancient inquiry into the structure of metaphor was less resourceful than ours, it was not I dare say because Aristotle was less intelligent than the best modern critics. Our multiverse has increasingly, since the seventeenth century, consisted of unstable objects dissolving into energy; and there has been no limit to the extension of analogy. Criticism follows whatever it is given to follow. Are the famous lucidity and restraint of the Greeks evidence that by nature they were more lucid and more restrained than we? I doubt it. For even the physical sight may be controlled by the religious selectivity, which fixes the height and the direction of the casement framing our inspection of the world. To introduce at the end of an essay, so large and undeveloped a conception is an impropriety of length and occasion; I offer it as historical relativism in defense of Longinus and of ourselves.

On no kind of literature is Longinus as searching as Aristotle on tragedy. But I risk the guess that he came nearer to a comprehensive theory of literary form than any other ancient critic. If he did not quite make the leap to a complete theory of the language of imagination, we must remember that nobody in the ancient world did. He shared Aristotle's cosmetic sense of the simple relation between word and thing; in a world of fixed forms, thing was unyielding; the word, like its object, retained a plastic visibility. With the Greeks the "transference" of "names" was limited to the surface designation, to the comparison of objects in the round, to sculpturesque analogy. Metaphor was a feature of discourse to be described, not a metaphysical problem to be investigated. We need not see as a personal limitation Longinus's failure to investigate a problem that for him did not exist. The permanent critics do not settle the question. They compel us to ask it again. They are the rotating chairmen of a debate only the rhetoric of which changes from time to time. Among these we may think of Longinus, if we will read him not in our age, but in his own.

—1948

A SUPPRESSED PREFACE
to a Collection of Poems

A WHILE ago I began to see that if I lived long enough I
should at last get out of a few scattered books of verse a single
book, that at intervals of about ten years had been brought up to
date. In *Selected Poems* (1937) was all the verse that I thought
readable up to that time, if anybody wanted to read it. The present collection contains the poems from that book and a few
written since which I should wish to survive me (if one may
glance publicly at that improbability); and one does not get any
younger. The reader may see on the title-page the phrase "A
Selection"; it will probably appear on the title-page of the last
collection that I may be able to persuade some publisher to take
on if I live to be eighty and write verse to the end. But I see no
reason why anybody should write verse to the end.

It has seemed to me very nearly impossible for an American
poet today to write verse through a long life, as Thomas Hardy
wrote it, out of a cheerful belief in philosophic "pessimism," or
as some American poets have tried of late to write it, with a sad
thump of the tub which one would guess from the sound, contained chiefly the hollows of an invisible utopia. But the defects
of my contemporaries do not excuse my own, which are perhaps of the same, perhaps of a different order. I could doubtless
point, not to the absence of a consistent "interest" in a book cov-
ering twenty-five years, but to the probable presence of one. Yet
if it is here, I do not know what it is. It is not a political or, in
any developed sense, a philosophical interest; nor a bias that a
Christian (even a Christian poet) would acknowledge as religious. Yet in its "historical influences" what I have written about
in this book cannot be altogether outside the Christian experience; but what the Christian experience is I do not know; only
Christians can know it.

Many years ago I wrote a tract against the conscious and the
obsessed uses of the will in poetry: I thought that the will made

poets mistake what ought to be for what may be; I suspected these poets, as I suspected myself, and still do, because I could not see in them or in me enough probability. I have tried not to know too much about what I wanted the world to be; I can only envy the men who, just before the atomic age, knew more than I did about what the world was going to be. As R. E. Lee said of himself, I was "always wanting something," but what I occasionally thought I wanted had very little chance of success: I could not think it had more. That slight chance appears in these poems (to ear and eye) at a distance. There is perhaps a real difference between the men who think about what they cannot get and those who, like myself, think about what they have not got. I frequently wish that I had "America" (a subject for sociology and conversation) but I haven't even got the few hundred square miles of it that I have been able to see; I have not got "Democracy" (a subject discussed by amateur theologians) and I have not got its popular enemy, who changes his initials every few years.

I hope that in the midst of these serious privations one may be allowed intermittences of unease. For these are certain; and to 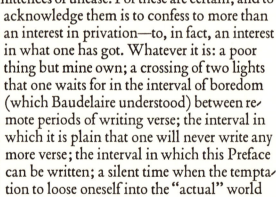 acknowledge them is to confess to more than an interest in privation—to, in fact, an interest in what one has got. Whatever it is: a poor thing but mine own; a crossing of two lights that one waits for in the interval of boredom (which Baudelaire understood) between remote periods of writing verse; the interval in which it is plain that one will never write any more verse; the interval in which this Preface can be written; a silent time when the temptation to loose oneself into the "actual" world and to deny the poor reality that one suspects to exist, would lead to selfviolence in men who have no talent for actuality.

—1946